# CLARENCE·DARROW
## the journeyman
### lessons for the modern lawyer

Mike Papantonio

A SEVILLE SQUARE BOOK
Pensacola, Florida

Also by Mike Papantonio

*In Search of Atticus Finch—*
*A motivational book for lawyers*

FOR
TERRI AND SARA,
WHO HAVE TAUGHT ME TO PAY ATTENTION
TO WHAT REALLY MATTERS

## A SEVILLE SQUARE BOOK

**Seville Publishing**
*Correspondence:*
>Post Office Box 12308
>Pensacola, Florida 32581
*Offices:*
>316 South Baylen
>Fourth Floor
>Pensacola, Florida 32501

CLARENCE DARROW, THE JOURNEYMAN
LESSONS FOR THE MODERN LAWYER
FIRST SEVILLE SQUARE EDITION, JULY 1997
>EDITORIAL ASSISTANCE AND BOOK DESIGN: SONNY BREWER
>COVER DESIGN: CYNTHIA TURNER

ISBN 0-9649711-1-9

Seville Square Books may be obtained for educational,
seminar, or promotional use in bulk quantities at discount
rates. For information, please write to:
**Promotional Department, Seville Publishing,
Post Office Box 12308, Pensacola, Florida 32581**

## ACKNOWLEDGEMENTS

JOHN ACUFF

WAYNE ALFORD

TODD ALLEY

KEN BAILEY

DIANA BAILEY

BILL BAKER

BOBBY BLANCHARD

JOHN BRAY

MICHAEL BRICKMAN

ANDY CHILDERS

NICK DITTMAR

KIM EVERS

CHARLES GIBSON

ROSS GOODMAN

BEN GORDON

JAMES HALEY

DAVID HALBERG

PAT KEAHEY

ARCHIE LAMB

MARTIN LEVIN

TERRI LEVIN

CONNIE MINNICK

JOHN MORGAN

LARRY MORRIS

JOHN ROMANO

HERB SADLER

CYNTHIA TURNER

# INTRODUCTION

My first book, *In Search of Atticus Finch,* paid tribute to the great fictional lawyer, Atticus Finch, from Harper Lee's *To Kill a Mockingbird.* The premise of my book was that lawyers in the '90s could learn how to improve their quality of life by adopting from Atticus some of his approach to life and lawyering.

Atticus Finch appeared, at least to me, to be a truly decent human being who simply chose to practice law in the same way he lived his life:

honorably, with sensitivity, care, and intellectual honesty; with inspired wisdom and enlightenment.

The advantages of lawyering with wisdom and enlightenment are the focus of this book. A different role model, however, will be used. Our role model is Clarence Darrow, who, unlike Atticus, was flesh-and-blood real. Unlike Atticus, Darrow was "blessed" with an abundance of human flaws and shortcomings. He was dealt a hand that any modern lawyer could have been dealt. His struggles were as real and complex as our own.

History books give us plenty of facts and details about Clarence Darrow. Biographers tell us about his parents, where he lived, where he was educated, how he lawyered, when he died. In the fifty books written about the man, no stone has been left unturned. We've been given all the "facts" we could possibly want to know about Darrow. But this is not a history book or a biography.

This book is devoted to the spiritual journey of a professed agnostic. This book aims to shed some light on his personal gospels, the axioms, and the principles he lived by that still prop up the name of Clarence Darrow—decades after his death. Clarence Darrow learned some basic, universal truths about living and lawyering in his eighty-one years. This book explores those truths and places them in the context of lawyering in the '90s.

Anyone who has read one or more of the fifty books written about Clarence Darrow would probably conclude that Darrow, throughout his life, worked hard to broaden and deepen his knowledge and understanding of the world in which he lawyered. He traveled down a path toward wisdom and enlightenment that might seem like an unnecessary struggle to many lawyers today. In his autobiography, Darrow comments that he visualized his life as a journey, an evolution of the spirit. Darrow analyzed his journey first in terms of how he evolved within the broad community of mankind, and, second, by how he evolved as a lawyer within that community.

Clarence Darrow at seventy-two was still declaring that he was agnostic. His short and not-very-well-known book of essays *Why I Am an Agnostic and Other Essays* is, to many who read it, a curiosity. The criticism of organized religious beliefs is shrill, flippant, and bordering on sophomoric tirade. The essence of Darrow's attack is, one might say: "If you cannot see it, there is nothing there." Darrow would not place his trust in something that could not be seen or touched or understood logically.

It would, however, have been more broad-minded and sensible for Darrow to declare that while he rejects the mystery of faith, and the trappings and ceremony of religion, he still embraces the wisdom that the religious traditions offer.

For example, the Hebrew prophets Amos and Isaiah had a straightforward message for their people. They told them that the enlightened man, the wise man, is not the keeper and dispenser of arcane, esoteric secrets, but rather lives his life by unthinkably simple formulas:

*Learn to love your neighbor.*
*Learn to do good.*
*Spend your life promoting justice.*
*Do all you can for the oppressed.*
*Be just to the orphan.*
*Plead the case of the widow.*
*Do not ignore the disadvantaged.*
*Show humility as you serve others.*

The truth is that Darrow spent most of his life following Isaiah's and Amos's simple formula for enlightened living in spite of the fact that it was delivered by religious prophets.

The nihilist side of Darrow forced him to personally sift and sort through the experiences of his life and choose for himself the insights and truths he would live by. Struggle, not divine direction, characterized Darrow's journey toward wisdom. He wanted it that way. Truths seldom unfolded for Darrow easily. He seemed most happy when he could beat his fists against the stars.

This book does not completely buy into Darrow's method for finding inspired wisdom. It is the goal of this book to "get home" by another way. Will Rogers pointed out many years ago that experience alone is a hard way to learn when we can so easily borrow from the insights and revelations already discovered by those who journeyed before us.

Waging battles to win what is truth may indeed build depth in character. Socrates was convinced, however, that what dominates the journey toward enlightenment and wisdom is *desire*. Given sufficient desire—"equal to the desire to breathe"—enlightenment of the mind may be acquired not with fierce struggle, but by listening with all one's ability to truth when it is offered. Darrow did not embrace that philosophy. Most of the time, in fact, he turned a deaf ear to the advice offered by those who had gone before him. He loved the battle too much to allow anyone to do his fighting for him.

Throughout this book we will plot a course to the same destination that Darrow sought, that of wisdom and enlightenment, but we will take a different tack from Darrow, who sailed his "untried bark across an angry sea." We will seek calmer seas. We will cast off on well-tried vessels. If Isaiah, Amos, Buddha, Mohammed, Confucius, Solomon, Jesus, or Hindu Scripture offers suggestions about becoming wise, or enlightening our lives, or nurturing our spirit, we will examine what they have to say. We will not turn a deaf ear. We will not jump ship and drown ourselves when they willingly advise us where the water is cold, dark, and deep.

Huston Smith is a modern philosopher and theologian. He has spent most of his adult life studying the world's great religions. Smith suggests that all religions from Islam to Buddhism to Christianity offer similar advice for achieving inspired wisdom and enlightened living even though they might dress it up differently.

Organized religion does not "hold title" to the truth. Religious traditions *borrow* the truths they teach. Truth is universal, belonging to all of us equally—not to any one ethnic people, not to any one culture, not to any one era of history. Smith refers to these truths as *wisdom traditions.* Smith says, "If we take the world's religions at their best, we discover the distilled wisdom of the human race."

This "distilled wisdom" that Smith refers to as the wisdom traditions provides instruction that has the potential—if we pay attention—to help us become better lawyers and better people.

Darrow got there on his own, but that does not mean we must do the same. We are free to accept the help that the wisdom traditions offer. In fact, we are living in an era of lawyering when we cannot afford to spend our lifetime figuring out what Darrow fought so long and hard to figure out. The American public has lost its patience with us. We must learn quickly. Darrow was viewed by his public as a champion of justice. In his lifetime, he was a folk hero to millions of Americans. Labels like "champion of justice" and "folk hero" would find few takers among Americans regarding the typical lawyer today.

Sol M. Linowitz, in his book *The Betrayed Profession,* gives lawyers a powerful wake-up call about why we must become wiser and more enlightened about how we live and lawyer. First, Linowitz insightfully makes a case for the idea that virtually every aspect of our society depends on a healthy ethical, moral, and service-oriented judicial structure. In other words, what has lurked in the corner of our minds all along since we graduated from law school is true: what we do from day to day *really does matter.* In that same breath, Linowitz tells us that America's judicial framework is not healthy. He tells us that it is not service oriented and is on shaky ground ethically and morally. Linowitz says:

> *The most frightening measure of what the legal professional has lost is that most Americans do not even remember the trust that society once placed in its lawyers. If a new Alexis de Tocqueville came to America today to study its laws and customs, he could never come up with the idea that the lawyers were the country's natural aristocracy.*

*Lawyers blame the law schools, the law schools blame the lawyers, the judges blame the lawyers, the lawyers say the clients (or their sense that they must go the limit for their clients) made them do it. Others blame the culture: It's a jungle out there; ethical standards are down wherever you look. Wall Street brokers who hold themselves out as agents trade for their own account to their client's disadvantage. Even the clergy seem more prone to scandal than they used to be. Why single out lawyers for the loss of ethical fibre at a time when ethical decline is so widespread? Because lawyers are supposed to be the custodians of a community's legal and ethical sense.*

The journey that is recommended in this book is not one that needs to be made simply because it might improve your life alone. If Linowitz is right, that we are "the custodians of a community's legal and ethical sense," we owe it to that community to begin to *consider*, at least, a journey beyond where we presently stand. It is time to look for higher ground.

We owe it to ourselves and to our communities to analyze what made Darrow look different from all of us. We owe it to ourselves and to our communities to pay attention to the wisdom offered by ancient sages, who were not looking for self-aggrandizement, but who wanted to help us improve our lives *so that* we might also improve the lives of others, and they might improve the lives of others, and so on. We cannot afford to fear sounding too much the do-gooder, or Pollyannaish, when we say that what we do as lawyers matters deeply to the society in which we live.

Theodore Koskoff, an immensely respected trial lawyer from Connecticut, wrote the following words several years before his death in 1989.

*If you are a lawyer, then what are you?*

*If you are a lawyer, you stand between the abuse of governmental power and the individual.*

*If you are a lawyer, you stand between the abuse of judicial power and the individual.*

*If you are a lawyer, you are the hair shirt to the smugness and complacency of society.*

*If you are a lawyer, you are helping to mold the rights of individuals for generations to come.*

*In short, if you are a lawyer, you are the Trustee of our liberties.*

These words may sound too "touchy-feely" to carry much weight for the cynic who tends to overintellectualize. People who knew Koskoff, however, recognized that he walked his talk and spent his life acting as a "custodian of the community's legal and ethical sense." Those words meant something to him, and were not just another piece of calligraphy, matted and framed for his office wall.

In the title of this book, Clarence Darrow is referred to as a *journeyman*. Typically, a journeyman is someone who has moved beyond apprenticeship and is in training to become a master at his craft. Darrow recognized that lawyering is a craft that, if mastered, requires more than average wisdom and enlightenment. Like the master carpenter who is distinguished from the merely "good" carpenter because of a kind of artistry inherent in his work, Darrow set himself apart from the lawyering crowd whose work might have been good, but lacked true mastery.

The term *journeyman* may be ascribed to Darrow because he is a man who valued wisdom and enlightenment above anything he could possess or own in a material world. He practiced his craft in a way that required him to constantly expand, improve, and upgrade his understanding of people, places, and ideas. Engaged in near-constant study and reflection, and continually seeking experiences to underscore his learning, he was able to move from apprenticeship to mastery. It was a journey that required sacrifice, selflessness, and a strong belief that through wisdom he could do better for himself and the people whose lives he touched. He could do better by rejecting the image of lawyering handed down to him by generations of lawyers before him. He could do better by roaming the periphery of the crowd, by not accepting the crowd's definition of lawyering, by finding his own path to success as he alone defined it. "Custodian of the community's legal and ethical sense" was an honor far more appealing to him than being "the richest, most powerful lawyer in the country."

There are tens of thousands of Darrow-like Journeymen in our ranks today. It is my hope that this book makes it to your hand, and that by reading it you are reminded that what you do really matters—that your grace, your enlightened lawyering, and your insight and wisdom are needed by the "community" now more than ever.

*The only safety of man
is to cultivate [reason] and
extend his knowledge so that he
will be sure to understand life.*

—*Clarence Darrow*

# PART ONE

## AN OVERVIEW

A person who has learned a trade, who is no longer an apprentice and not yet a master is sometimes referred to as a journeyman. A journeyman might describe his level of skill and knowledge as "good," "reliable," or "competent," but not yet "masterful." He is, after all, still learning. A journeyman might be described by his peers as being capable and consistently dependable but one who is still working hard and to the best of his ability toward becoming a master of his trade. The journeyman is committed to doing the "heavy lifting," the hard work that is required to get to where he wants to go, to achieve the skills and knowledge to take him there.

The complexity of progressing from apprenticeship to the level of journeyman and on to mastery obviously varies according to the type of job or skill the journeyman is attempting to master. However difficult the task, each trade—from carpenter to electrician, from brewer to baker—has a system that helps the journeyman bridge the gap between apprentice and master.

The role lawyers play in improving the quality of life within their communities is at least as important as the improvements brought by electricians, carpenters, and other members of the "journeyman trades." Poorly performed lawyering skills are equally as dangerous to the community members' well-being as poorly performed skills in the building trades. If an unskilled, inefficient, unfit carpenter fails to properly frame a new house, there is a considerable risk that the entire structure may be forever unsound. The house could also fall down. The deficient, inadequate, talent of that carpenter and his poor workmanship can lead to consequences ranging from inconvenience to financial loss to injury or even death.

Likewise, there are possible dire consequences when the lawyer is "incomplete," "unfinished," "artless," or "undeveloped" in his skills as advocate or counsel. Lawyering like this is mere meddling and dabbling with the lives of people who live in our community. The consequences range from injustice to naked corruption, from loss of liberty to loss of life. Someone, at some time, will pay for the harm that is done by the "abridged version" of a lawyer loose in the world.

Clarence Darrow was the unabridged, complete-edition lawyer. He began his lawyering life as an apprentice and became a master, or in the term applied in this book, a Sage. It was not an easily gained rise to the top, however. Throughout most of his life he dedicated himself to the heavy lifting and hard work that is characteristic of the Journeyman. William James said it is the "slow dull heave of the will" that accomplishes transformation to enlightenment or wisdom. Darrow was not content to be an incomplete, unfinished, underdeveloped lawyer. He therefore consistently applied his will toward his own betterment. He believed he owed his clients the fullest dimension of insight and skill he could reasonably offer. What he gained in wisdom and insight as a Journeyman was a lasting benefit to his friends, family, peers, and clients. He improved their lives by enlightening and illuminating his own.

Darrow did not rely on or wait for some mystical divine spark to set him on his way and guide him along as a Journeyman. Agnostics don't often feel "divine sparks." His spiritual journey was not mystical, mysterious, or other-worldly. He became a complete package, an enlightened lawyer, through his own hard work and diligence.

Outsiders by the busload would have the world believe that a lawyer doesn't have a spiritual bone in his body to enlighten or illuminate. They would argue that any journey attempted by a lawyer toward spiritual enlightenment would be like bailing a sinking boat with a fisherman's net. We know that such an indictment is itself full of holes.

The very fact that there is such a misunderstanding about who and what we are as lawyers, however, makes it pretty clear that something is awry.

Perhaps the "system" has developed its own agenda that makes it difficult for lawyers to honor their individual spiritual needs. Maybe the system has taken on a purpose all its own that now has little or nothing to do with spiritual journeys or enlightened living. What if it is the system that forces us to pay too much respect to accumulating personal wealth and power? What if it is the *system* that has led us to a place of such impersonal values that core values are swallowed up and spat out—a place where spirituality, enlightenment, and wisdom simply don't figure into the bottom line? Worse yet, what if this mysterious, labyrinthine thing we call the *system* is really a few hundred thousand fat cats with briefcases and law degrees "just passing through," grabbing what they can in the process?

As you read these pages there are attorneys who are your opponents who want to outwork you, outsmart you, outmaneuver you, and generally overburden you. They desperately want something you or your clients own or possess. There are, right now, judges who are not interpreting the law the same way you do and it will cost your client money at best, his liberty at worst. Within the next three weeks, you have two trials set on the docket and two major briefs due. Your children have begun calling you by your first name, as they do others who only drop by for a visit. And—by the way—your office manager is crying louder than ever for more things with which to "properly" run your law office. What you have is your share of wolves, big and bad, who want to huff and puff and blow your house down.

And now comes the author of this book, who wants you to spend your valuable time and energy thinking about concepts as "whimsical" as spirituality and enlightenment. Why in the name of a twenty-hour work day would one take on more work—especially this "nebulous" work of the Journeyman?

The answer is that there are tangible benefits to the Journeyman's effort. It can help you be a better, more effective, lawyer. There are ideas that Darrow understood and put to good use in this life as a lawyer. We can learn from this wisdom stuff of the great religions how to lawyer better right in the middle of a busy lawyering day. We can take what we learn home with us, to our families, and into our communities. The wolves at the door will still be huffing and puffing, but the journeyman "brickwork" we will be doing could save our hides. We simply need to decide we have the time and desire to do it. With that part done, we must then recognize that there are a few impediments, a few road blocks that stand between us and where we need to go in the course of our journey.

## Life in the Survival Lane

Too often, we retreat into what can be called a "survival mode." This mode is typified by an extremely well-focused state of mind where we narrow our vision and devote all of our creative energies to the task at hand, which is, of course, to stay in business and ensure at least a modicum of growth in that business. A survival-mode mindset does not lend itself well to risk taking. It is a mode that does not permit us to steal our attention from the role of task master.

Michael Brickman, a busy lawyer in Charleston puts it this way:

> *Thoroughbred race horses are trained to run around in circles at a high speed. They keep it up from the time they are colts until they are put out to pasture. The oval track becomes their entire world while they are competing. If it ever occurs to a race horse to get off the track and run over the mountains and through the wilderness, around trees and streams, they soon remember that their oats are back at the barn.*

Our "oval track" as lawyers is this survival mode we have created for ourselves. As we run around that track we fail to pay much attention to what's on the periphery—the mountains and streams, so to speak. Meaningful progress toward "enlightened living" seems whimsical, something that exists in rarefied mountain air too far removed from the oval track that we call home to be of any worthwhile consequence.

For many lawyers it is difficult to see any relationship whatsoever between renewing the spirit and the business of successful lawyering. Many of those in our ranks are content—in fact, thrilled—to stay squarely in the race and be judged only according to where they finish compared to the rest of the pack by the end of their careers. It is the only life as a lawyer that they know.

Lawyers have created a success ethic and an image that, when "properly and diligently" pursued, tends to gobble up the best parts of our lives. We work hard to pass that success ethic down from one generation of lawyers to the next. Kim Evers has practiced law for six years. She has coined a phrase that accurately describes what generation after generation of lawyers has passed on to each other. She calls it *image preservation.*

> *From the first day I started practicing law, all my orientation about successful lawyering came from silver-haired movers and shakers who had struggled for decades before me clenching their fists to grab more of the "good life." The image of these overbearing, status-seeking lawyer types looking for immortality through power, wealth, and possessions has become almost a cliché.*

> *I soon learned that my definition of what is a good life was dramatically different from theirs. The money was great, the accolades and recognition were pleasing, but financial status and "image preservation" do not lend themselves to personal growth or to much of a commodity called serenity or inner peace.*

## A BROADER VISION AND HIGHER SIGHTS

Robert Pirsig wrote a book called *Zen and the Art of Motorcycle Maintenance*, which the *New York Times Book Review* declared to be "arguably the most influential book of popular philosophy in recent times." It has become a classic even though almost two hundred publishers rejected the manuscript. It is an intriguing and provocative motorcycle journey through the "high country of the mind." The motorcyle Pirsig really wants to tune up is not the Harley his protagonist rides. It is the "motorcycle called *self.*"

The reason *Zen and the Art of Motorcycle Maintenance* has not gone out of print in twenty-two years is that the topic of better tuning ourselves is perennially in demand—for some, at least. For many, "image preservation" loses its power as a prime motivator in a short time, especially as one's vision begins to clear, or as we begin to "awaken," so to speak.

Our machines are strained and overdriven in the survival mode. Nonetheless, it is hard to rest and still pay attention to our practices. Thankfully, the Journeyman's work does not require a sabbatical to a mountain retreat. Neither are we required to chant mantras to overcome impediments to spiritual progress. The prophet Mohammed said to strive for enlightenment and wisdom, but tie your camel first. Farmers keep tending the crops, weavers keep making rugs, lawyers keep lawyering. We are not called upon to turn loose our camel and wander off into the desert. As a matter of fact, our first priority is to keep our lawyering fixed securely in our sights. Not only should we not leave our profession, but our profession stands to reap plentiful rewards from the "self" tuning we do, as will our own effective practice of the law.

The fine tuning of self—the movement toward the inner work that is recommended in this book—is achieved right in our own backyards. There is no call to a functional understanding of mystical or mysterious teachings, of complicated or arcane concepts. The premise of the book, in fact, is quite simply to abandon "image preservation" and become your highest and best self. The inner work this book will discuss can be summarized as follows:

1. *Become a Journeyman.*
2. *Start living and lawyering in a way that is consistent with the concept of "right livelihood."*
3. *Understand and admit how unhealthy ego turns your life upside-down.*
4. *Reward yourself by becoming a Servant.*
5. *Teach what you have learned and are learning.*
6. *Think and behave like a Sage.*

Each of the foregoing points will be the subject of a section in the book. We will develop more fully a preview of these ideas in the next few pages.

## RIGHT LIVELIHOOD

Huston Smith, in his book *World's Religions— A Guide to Our Wisdom Traditions,* explains why the Koran has been described as "a manual for businessmen." Smith tells how the Koran on the one hand is a roadmap for the spiritual journey of the faithful Muslim, while on the other it does not disallow or condemn "profit motive, economic competition, or entrepreneurial initiatives."

The Koran, however, demands that the Muslim pay constant attention to his spirituality; he must at all times balance competition with fair play. The merchant is entitled to his profit, but not at the expense of abandoning the core values he has been taught as a Muslim. The Koran counsels the businessman to conduct his trade according to the same values he would apply as a husband, a father, a friend, or a member of the community he serves. Or, in the words of John Morgan, a lawyer in Orlando, Florida:

> *I have often thought that it would be a good idea to scrap the standard, old, worn-out ethics classes taught in most law schools and, instead, make it mandatory for law students to read and discuss children's stories like* Aesop's Fables *and* Pinocchio. *They*

*clearly show what wrong looks like, how it feels and sounds. From these simple tales we can learn all we need to know about ethics: Do not cheat, do not lie; do not hurt others; show compassion—all the important stuff is there.*

*For instance, in* Pinocchio, *Jiminy Cricket had the responsibility of being the voice of conscience for Pinocchio while the puppet was working to become human, to become a real little boy. The arrangement between the cricket and the puppet did not work out well and it was clear that if Pinocchio was to become a real little boy, he would have to do the hard work of developing his conscience all on his own. A cricket was not going to be able to make the tough calls for Pinocchio.*

*In my own law practice, some days I feel like things will have a happy ending as they did for Pinocchio when he succeeded in becoming a human being. Other days I feel like Pinocchio the wooden puppet, and would gladly give the tough calls to a cricket. Like Pinocchio, however, I know that only I can do and say what must be done in order to "do the right thing." I, like the tiny hero in the children's story, must let* my *conscience be my guide.*

*I don't believe that any DR or EC discussed in law school more effectively illuminated the simple principle of conscience-guided choices.*

*On the contray, some of the DRs and ECs included in our codes of professional responsiblity seem to suggest a duality of conscience, with one for use in our law offices, and another for use everywhere else. Honoring the whispered advice from one conscience is difficult enough, but bouncing between two becomes impossible.*

Mohammed did not have sole claim on the idea that we must mesh our work with all other parts of our life. Buddhists, too, study the concept of "right livelihood," to discern the importance of consistent values both inside and outside the workplace. The Buddha, in compiling his list of steps toward enlightenment, took a very rational view of a person's occupation, and the amount of time and energy it consumes in a waking day. He taught that there is no way a person can overcome the sheer weight of a profession that does not feed the spirit in significant ways. According to Buddha it is not possible to live an enlightened life and make a living at a job that compromises core values like honesty.

In Part Two of this book, "Right Livelihood," Clarence Darrow is seen bringing his passion for ideas into his office and the courtroom, thereby establishing a consistent value system "on the job" and off. He was not a wooden puppet for the system at one moment and a conscience-guided human being at other moments. He did not vacillate in a duality of conscience. In *The Story of My Life*, Darrow said:

> *In life one cannot eat his cake and have it, too; he must make his choice and then do the best he can to be content to go the way his judgment leads.*

## OVERCOMING AN UNHEALTHY EGO

In Sufi literature, ego is called the "commanding self" and is described as a mixture of primitive and conditioned responses common to everyone. Sufis say ego inhibits and distorts human progress and understanding. Cautions abound against ego, from religious and secular sources too numerous to count. Any journey to wisdom must, obviously, get past this commanding self. Clarence Darrow said it is easy to get caught in "the stresses and storms that are always merely incidental to existence" and forget what is truly important. The ego incidental to our human nature is a storm of unmeasured fury, and the "image preservation" it rages to maintain is absolutely antithetical to living an enlightened life.

Thomas M. Reavley sits as Senior Circuit Judge for the United States Court of Appeals for the Fifth Circuit. He served on the Texas Supreme Court between 1968 and 1977. An article written by Judge Reavley appeared in the *Texas Tech Law Review* in 1996. In it, Reavley offers his thoughts on why the spiritual journey away from ego is particularly important for lawyers and judges:

> *Ego, self at the center of it all, self exposed to praise and censure: that is the most common threat to our happiness and satisfaction. It bars good relations with others, anchors our abuses of ambition, and eats at our feelings. Only by getting outside and beyond self, only by caring for people and causes, only by catching the gleam of a distant horizon and responding to a stirring song, only above sordid selfishness can we find it all worthwhile. We were made for a better life. . . . Ah, ego. There is the snare, our misdirection and betrayer. No matter what our work or station, it bestrides, it bestrides us to make fools of us and undo our good works.*

Many lawyers and judges find it easy to remain fat, dumb, and happy at a level of character development that evolves around a distorted ego. They have both feet firmly planted in a superficial world that revolves around paying tribute to their wealth, their positions, their influence and power. Transcending this stage would be hard work, indeed. So why bother? In Part Three we consider the advantages of abandoning an unhealthy ego, this thing that Thomas Reavley calls the "most common threat to our happiness and satisfaction."

## AFTER THE EGO, THE JOURNEYMAN

There is a philosophical concept for which we don't have a good English word. It is *"the knowledge of a lack."* An illustration would be social activist students from the local college going out to stir up low-paid farmworkers who, beforehand, had been content with their wages. Now they have knowledge of their unfair wages. Now they want something better.

Before the Journeyman lawyer can take hold of that "something better," she must develop that knowledge of a lack. This can be extremely difficult to come by in a "successful" lawyer's world that seems, on the surface, to lack very little. All the possessions, wealth, power, and influence cloud the ability to feel a lack, to feel in any way incomplete, unfinished, or under-developed. Ken Bailey, a product liability lawyer from Houston, Texas, offers these thoughts:

*Several decades ago we were "counselors" instead of attorneys, lawyers, or advocates. To speak of someone as a counselor conjures up an image of wisdom, of someone worldly and full of insight, of knowledge that is both broad and deep, of someone who knows what the client does not.*

*Most lawyers today have forgotten what it takes to be a counselor in the fullest sense of the word, including the requirement to be also philosopher, theologian, poet, warrior, scientist, and historian.*

*If we are to become, once again, "counselors," then we must continually evolve and grow in our understanding of ourselves and the world around us. We must improve ourselves, and commit to the process of a positive personal transformation, so that we may assist others in improving*

*their own lives. We must seek to become
counselors again.*

Clarence Darrow was a counselor's counselor,
studying and lecturing on topics ranging from
physics to sociology. He garnered the admiration and respect of the greatest thinkers of his
day. His knowledge of the law was comple-
mented by an equal knowledge of philosophy
and theology. Darrow's career produced more
than fifty magazine articles, from "Robert
Burns" and "Schopenhauer" to "The Divorce
Problem" and "Why Was God So Hard on
Women and Snakes?" He penned more than
twenty essay/pamphlets on matters as diverse
as "The Rights and Wrongs of Ireland" and "Leo
Tolstoi" to "Why I Am an Agnostic" and "War
Prisoners." At least nine full-length books (two
with co-authors) were written by Darrow. If
for no other reason than the output from his
pen, Clarence Darrow does not resemble most
practicing lawyers in America today. Half a
hundred or so books have been written *about* the
man. Without exception he embodied each of the
attributes that we ascribe to the Journeyman. Part

Four explores the ambitious and gratifying path taken by the Journeyman, which is open to every lawyer. Part Four also tells us why the trip is worth the effort.

## A HEART FOR SERVICE

The role of Servant emerges from growth that begins during the Journeyman stage, which is itself, of course, a continuous and lifelong stage. The Journeyman becomes a Servant when he places an increasing emphasis on others—when purpose and direction begins to move away from "me first."

The Servant more often and more consistently places the needs of others, and the well-being of the greater community in which he lives and lawyers, ahead of his own self-gratification and self-aggrandizement. Then, as a result of abandoning a "me-first, me-only" mentality, the Journeyman lawyer begins to have a lasting, positive impact in the world of family, friends, and clients. Sometimes other-centered service "catches fire" and spreads far beyond its point of origin. Too rarely, too inconsistently, are lawyers fueling the blaze. Too often, instead, our lawyering kin occupy the media headlines with stories of *dis*service born out of their self-seeking motives. When we examine those motives to discover the impediments to genuine service, often we find that establishing and hanging on to "image" is a highlighted item. If service is *giving,* how is it that this business of serving others won't lose money for me? Consider the following observations from a lawyer who has practiced law for fifteen years.

> *I have spent a great deal of my career as a lawyer not fully grasping the direct relationship between giving and gain, that the two are inherently linked. Most of my interaction with my clients and peers, even my acquaintances, has too often found me focusing on what I could extract from them rather than what I could offer them. I have heard myself ask more times than I feel comfortable admitting, "What's in it for me?" I can clearly see that it is selfishness and cynicism and mistrust that drives my fear of being taken advantage of. It has been a big leap*

*for me to get to the strength one gets from*
*helping other people for nothing, for no pay,*
*for no return of favors; where there is noth-*
*ing in it for me.*

Clarence Darrow was completely "at the other end of the stick," claiming he could not avoid putting himself in the other person's place, that his sympathies always went out to the weak, the suffering, the poor. "Realizing their sorrows," said Darrow, "I tried to relieve them in order that I myself might be relieved." He so strongly identified with the hurting in others that he actually felt it within himself.

And as to the money consideration that so frequently blocks acting upon the empathy that we, in fact, might feel, Darrow said:

*I don't know the meaning of "success." To*
*some—perhaps to most—it means "money."*
*I never cared much for it, nor tried to get*
*much of it, or ever had a great deal, but still*
*most of my life I have had what I needed.*

It would be easy to file the foregoing under the heading of self-politicking that in itself speaks of a decidedly egotistical character. Except there is a far different proof in the pudding. The sheer number and variety of the people who turned out to pay their last respects at his funeral, the people he had served selflessly, they are the ones who speak loudest in Clarence Darrow's behalf. In Irving Stone's description in *Clarence Darrow for the Defense* it is clear that this was a man who lawyered to a different tune. The funeral parlor in Chicago, Stone wrote, stayed open for forty-eight hours straight while . . .

> *workingmen from the stockyards and steel mills in their overalls; scrubwomen in their Mother Hubbards; colored men with their lunch baskets under their arms; colored women [who brought children] to see the white man who had fought for their race; . . . the weak and confused and indeterminate ones who had been strengthened by his boldness and resolution; . . . the mentally ill, whose plight he had tried to make intelligible; teachers, whose freedom he had broadened by his*

*struggles; students whose minds had been stimulated by his iconoclasm; lawyers, to whose trade he had given another dimension; clergymen, to whom he had revealed Christianity at work; the labor leaders and union members whose organizations he had preserved under fire... all streamed past his coffin, all those who had needed a friend and had had no friend and to whom Clarence Darrow had been a friend.*

If one-tenth the practicing lawyers in America could earn one-tenth of the admiration and love that Clarence Darrow earned in his life of service to others, there would be a total rewrite of the value of our profession.

Interestingly enough, as we discuss in Part Five of this book, "The Servant," the good things that people accomplish for others are not even diminished when selfish motives drive the behavior.

## THE TEACHER

In one story of Prince Siddhartha Gautama's enlightenment, when 2,500 years ago he became the Buddha, it is said he perceived ultimate reality symbolized by a wheel. Curiously, the wheel in his vision was not turning. Then he understood: in order for the truth he had learned to assume its full dynamic potential, he must teach it to others. Until he did so it would remain static. Some Sages might be content to keep the truth in static self-possession.

E. A. Burtt, in *The Teachings of the Compassionate Buddha,* asked the question, "How could he make his discovery intelligible and persuasive to others, so that it might guide them also toward true happiness and peace?" Buddha hit upon the way, that much is obvious, for now Buddhism is one of the seven great religions of the world. In Part Six of this book, "The Teacher," our discussion turns to the Journeyman's obligation to teach others what he has learned and is continuing to learn himself, lessons that can help others improve their lives.

It is just as important for us, for different reasons, to teach others on the path of self-discovery and wisdom as it was for the Buddha. No one is trying to start a new religion, or even a new church. We have an adequate supply of both. Our motivation to teach is simply to help others realize that acting upon the deeper truths *they already know* will improve the quality of their lives and their lawyering beyond any other "self-help" program available.

What is supremely important and often quite surprising about the concept of teaching others is its "boomerang effect." What you teach comes back by a multiple of many to enlighten your own life: "A full measure, pressed down, shaken together, and running over, will be poured into your lap" is how Jesus put it. If you want to survive your lawyering career with your core values intact, you must teach others.

An article entitled "Civility" by Robert Josefsburg was reprinted in the January 1997 issue of the *Florida Bar Journal*. In that article, Josefsburg discusses the importance of teaching and mentoring within the legal profession. He says, "This is the most important thing you can do. And it has wonderful effects. Teach. Preach. Be a mentor." Then the author quotes a former practicing lawyer, who became dean of Notre Dame Law School:

> *When I graduated from law school twenty-nine years ago, people learned to practice law at the feet of a master. Lawyers would take you under their wing. . . . Even if you went into sole practice, there was someone in town to mentor to you and teach the practice of law. Inevitably what was taught was professionalism. . . . Somewhere along the line in the last thirty years, however, lawyering became more expensive. . . . Efficiency became a priority, and the mentoring system broke down. The seniors were pressured to increase their billable hours and could no longer afford to spend time with the young people coming in. In the meantime, no one was teaching practice or, incidentally, professionalism.*

In this book's treatment, professionalism is not incidental to teaching. It occupies the place of premier importance. The professionalism relevant within a context of wisdom, enlightenment and spirituality comes under the heading of "conscience-guided" lawyering. From the same *Florida Bar Journal* piece we just mentioned comes this quote: "When there are disagreements between your conscience and your client, always obey your conscience." Which, in the lawyering environment of the 1990s, is far easier said than done. That is why travelers on the path we discuss are Journeymen and not Masters. That is why we must help each other by teaching.

Also, in Part Six we will emphasize that you are teaching at every moment, and the lesson is *you*—as you are, without benefit of verbal eloquence and flashy rhetoric. People are more likely to remember what you say and do in the office break room than what they learn from your masterful orations broadcast from behind a lacquered hardwood podium.

## THE SAGE

Inner work marked by continued growth and development will lead, ultimately, to a stage that we will call the Sage, discussed in Part Seven. Solomon set a precedent in rising to this level of wisdom.

The Bible tells us that God asked Solomon, "What would you like me to give you?" Solomon, having the choice of anything his heart could desire, chose instead of wealth or a long life "a heart to understand how to discern between good and evil." God was very pleased with Solomon's request and told him that he would grant him a discerning judgment "wise and shrewd as none before you." In our discussion of the Sage, we will see that his wisdom serves him on a daily basis in very practical ways, helping him not so much in "how to discern between good and evil" as in, for instance, identifying the traps we fall into regarding our attitude toward ownership and possessions. It has become clear to the Sage that a bigger personal inventory of "stuff" does not lead to real fulfillment and is not the silver bullet for happiness.

We will see, too, that the Sage is one who puts a higher priority on keeping a broad enough margin in his lawyering life to allow room for the pursuit and enjoyment of simple pleasures, like creating private moments for himself—right in the middle of busy working day.

## A BEACON ON THE HORIZON

The enlightened living that comes from wisdom is the object of our quest in this book. You will not become wise nor your life enlightened by reading this or a thousand other books with a similar theme. But we can raise our level of awareness of the importance of the breadth and depth of knowledge wisdom is heir to, its advantages and usefulness to us as lawyers and men and women interacting within society. Awareness and awakening is the starting place on the road to wisdom.

## WHERE DID DARROW START?

Or, for that matter, where did Clarence Darrow go? We will come up with answers to those questions that will serve *you*, as you move along on your own journey beyond unhealthy ego to serving and teaching, to a livelihood that *matters* in the best sense of the word—to you, your family, your clients, and the entire community that thinks of you as "counselor."

A Persian proverb says: "It is ignorance to test that which has been tested." It is my aim to provide sources that have tested the value of undertaking inner work. We will gather knowledge from Darrow, from other lawyers, and from the best teachings of the world's religions. If we accomplish this book's objectives, we can establish a starting place on a reasonably well-lighted path to wiser and better lawyering, a path that Clarence Darrow made before us.

**"**

*Like most lawyers*
*who dare to think about*
*their profession,*
*I had for a number of years*
*viewed it with doubt and distrust.*

—*Clarence Darrow*

**"**

# PART TWO

## "RIGHT LIVELIHOOD"

C larence Darrow's writing suggests that he was at times not at all certain that he had chosen the right career for himself. Some days, Darrow wanted to be a writer, some days a scientist. Although history records his decision in favor of a law career, it would be inaccurate to conclude that Darrow had a genuine love for lawyers or lawyering.

### WHAT JOB IS THIS?

At times, Darrow spoke harshly of lawyers: "Lawyers still keep the poor in their place by jails and barbarous laws." Darrow even saw fit to belittle lawyers' avocational pursuits and abilities:

> *As a rule lawyers are not great readers; nor do they produce much literature; now and then a lawyer does write a good book, but it is rather seldom, and generally such a lawyer has abandoned law for literature; ordinarily, lawyers feel that literature should be avoided because it is too imaginative and absorbing.*

And in his essay on Voltaire, Darrow added:

> *Voltaire had genius, imagination, feeling, and poetry, and these gifts always have been, and always will be, incompatible with the practice of law.*

John P. Altgeld, Darrow's early mentor, no doubt influenced Darrow's attitudes about the profession of lawyering. There is a passage in his autobiography where Darrow describes Altgeld's decision to discontinue the practice of law after his career in politics had ended:

*He [Altgeld] did not want to go back to the bar to practice law; he had come to rather despise the profession; he felt that its strongest men sold themselves to destroy people, to perpetuate and intensify the poverty of the oppressed and enlarge their burdens.*

Both Altgeld and Darrow practiced law during a time in America when a few men, extremely rich and powerful figures in manufacturing, transportation, and commerce, had tremendous influence in America's political and judicial arena. They were the "haves" wielding their power to the detriment of the "have-nots." Most of the business of lawyers during that era truthfully was devoted to protecting the interests of the "haves."

In Clarence Darrow's day there existed a scant handful of lawyers who actually came to the aid of America's underclass and the disenfranchised. Those few lawyers were primarily union labor lawyers and criminal defense lawyers.

**WHEN LIFE AND LIVELIHOOD DON'T MATCH**
All the world's great religions teach that the vocation a man or woman chooses inescapably impacts the spiritual dimensions of that individual. One might ask how it could, in fact, be otherwise when the sheer time and energy demanded of any career is a force as inescapable as the pull of the moon on the earth's oceans.

For example, Buddhists believe that they have a solution for dealing with the ills and troubles of mankind through devotion to the steps on what is called the Eightfold Path. The fifth step on the Eightfold Path, very simply put, is that we should choose a vocation that can best be described as a "right livelihood."

Buddha went so far as to compile a list of occupations incompatible with improved spirituality, including those of tax collectors, arms makers, alcohol brewers, and prostitutes. Lawyers are not included in that list. Contrary to public perception, lawyers as individuals are just as spiritually inclined as anyone else. There are lawyers writing and lecturing today who suggest, however, that there is perhaps a widening gap between lawyers' private faith and their public practice. They say that attorney advocacy for the client has become too drenched with greed, is mean-spirited and characterized by lawyers' unhealthy love of power and influence.

Walk down the aisle of any bookstore and the titles alone of books about lawyers do anything but leave you with a warm and fuzzy feeling about how we make our living. *No Contest—Corporate Lawyers and the Perversion of Justice in America; Rascals: The Selling of the Legal Profession; The Betrayed Profession* . . . these are just a few of the many books suggesting that lawyering and Buddha's concept of right livelihood are not exactly joined at the hip. Fortunately, books about greedy, unscrupulous lawyers are not books about *all* lawyers, but about many who have lost their way. I would add, too, that the lawyers who are the subjects of these books are people who probably could not find a "right livelihood" in any profession. It's too bad they chose lawyering as a stopping-off place.

In Hindu scriptures, the idea that one has a moral and ethical duty to fulfill a social responsibility as one goes about making a living is described within a concept known as *dharma*. A person's ethical values in the workplace must be woven together with and become inseparable from his spiritual and religious faith and moral values.

The combined logic of the Buddhist belief in a "right livelihood" and the *dharma* of Hindu teaching is plainly simple to comprehend for any lawyer willing to pay attention. They articulate the obvious. While we may all to some extent separate our lives into subparts—family, career, leisure, and the like—it is impossible to make progress toward wisdom unless our core values guide us within all the areas of our lives. The way we conduct ourselves in our vocations, and the way we live and interact within our families, among our friends—and even our foes—functions within a continuum. "Right livelihood" is important to the Buddhist because the Buddhist believes that our spiritual life centers on what we think about—that we in fact *become* what we think about. If the manner in which we make a living requires that we endlessly and regularly make compromises between what is right and wrong, then our livelihood is a huge roadblock to finding much peace in our life. Schizophrenic attempts to be one person in the office and entirely another person at home around friends and family is not a very efficient way to live.

## "I YAM WHAT I YAM AND THAT'S ALL THAT I YAM." —*POPEYE*

It is not possible to compartmentalize our lives in such a way that we can dishonestly shred documents for a corporate client on Monday and honor the Torah, Bible, or Koran on Saturday or Sunday. All the religions advance guidelines about how we should live, and those guidelines are founded upon a premise that all aspects of our life are interconnected. Like it or not, what you are in your business suit is what you are at poolside. Wherever you go, you might say, there *you* are. You may wear different masks, manipulating your "front" to suit the occasion, but you have been blessed with only one spirit.

John Romano, a trial lawyer in Florida, offered his thoughts about what a right livelihood means to him:

*I saw an article in the newspaper last week. The headline read: "Tobacco Companies Had Lawyers Hide Health Risks, '64 Report Says." The article describes how lawyers participated in shredding documents, hiding scientific studies, and lying to the government about the incredible health risk caused by tobacco. No doubt they were paid their $500-per-hour Wall Street rate for prostituting themselves and my profession to a powerful corporate client. How have we arrived at a stage in our profession where to do such things is merely considered zealous representation?*

*Has it become part of our job description to knowingly plead the case of the fraud or the malingerer, collect the insurance money and whistle all the way to the bank? Have we lawyers now deluded ourselves into believing that we operate within some "higher calling," absolved of the most basic moral and ethical responsibilities toward society? Can we become lapdogs doing the bidding of corporate clients—who we know are legally, ethically, and morally wrong—simply for the sake of the profit margin?*

*There are dozens of intellectually flawed arguments for rationalizing dishonest ways of doing business. They have been handed down from generation to generation of lawyers who, in their turn, continue almost blindly, with great zeal, to represent every client who can afford to pay the fee. After my fifteen years of lawyering, those hand-me-down justifications seem tattered and worn.*

These thoughts of Romano's have been expressed in many different ways throughout the last two hundred years of lawyering. Elihu Root was a turn-of-the-century scholar of jurisprudence. He was also a Nobel Peace Prize winner. He is cited in dozens of appellate opinions as having spoken these words:

> *About half the practice of a decent lawyer is telling would-be clients that they are damned fools and should stop . . . the law lets you do it, but don't. It's a rotten thing to do.*

When we tell a client, partner, or associate that they are "damned fools and should stop," we are committing ourselves to decision making based on principle. That principle does not always further one's self-interest.

Barrows Dunham's 1971 book, *Ethics, Dead and Alive,* discussed decision making based on principle:

> *The proper mode of making decisions has the same principle as its source. One can (alas, one sometimes does!) decide on no wider ground than that of bare self-interest—or, if the act involved harm to others, of outright selfishness. To decide on such a ground is to ignore the worthiness of others, to regard one's own worthiness as exclusively important, to demand of*

> *others what one will not do oneself, or to refuse to do what one requires others to do. No rational ethics can be made of this. The heart of ethics is to decide by the one same principle that all other men are required to decide by. There are no exemptions; no one can get off the hook. And the habit, the trait of character, of deciding in this manner is "integrity."*

This principle-guided decision making is the same as the concept of *dharma* that guides the Hindu in his decisions. It is the cornerstone of "right livelihood" for the Buddhist. It is a simple and practical philosophy of accountability, which helps the world to work in a way that we as lawyers should want it to work. It contemplates that what we know in our heads and feel in our hearts and do with our hands should all be synthesized into an integrity that guides the whole. The interconnecting principle cannot be simply ignored; you cannot cavalierly exchange your prayer cloth, so to speak, for a document shredder as you enter the front door of your office.

Some might argue that lawyering somehow cannot, by its adversarial nature, ever be regarded and practiced as a right livelihood in a spiritual sense. If our life and law practice is up and running properly, however, then what we are doing will have a beneficial impact on the world around us. Our work will be right in every sense of the word.

What we do for a living really does matter and has the potential for powerful impact on the lives of many. Most lawyers know this. Most lawyers recognize, too, the responsibility to use their training, experience, and license to benefit the neglected, impoverished, oppressed, and disenfranchised within America's social, political, and economic arenas. Among the good lawyers, it is not simply some whimsical notion easily tossed off in exchange for a large fee.

## DARROW KEPT TO THE "HIGH ROAD"

Clarence Darrow describes a time in his life when he was hired as an attorney for the Chicago and North-Western Railway Company. Part of his responsibility was to represent the company in personal injury actions resulting from the company's negligence. Darrow writes:

> *I knew that the position was one that I should never really like. It was hard for me to take the side of the railroad company against one who had been injured in their service or against a passenger. I was aware that I always wanted the company to help them, and in this, my services were made easier by the general claim agent, Mr. Ralph C. Richards, whose sympathies were the same. I am sure that both he and I were able to help a great many people without serious cost to the road. Later, Mr. Richards gave up his position to inaugurate a great work for the prevention of accidents.*

During Darrow's time with the railroad, he was being paid more money than he had ever before made in his life. The position brought with it a great deal of professional recognition and respectability. Clarence Darrow had pushed himself to the front of the crowd, gaining money, power, and influence.

Darrow soon recognized, however, that his vision of lawyering and the commitments that came with that calling were much more complex for him. For him, there was more involved than simply leading the crowd. He had a notion that financial rewards, prestige, and all the trappings that came with position and power were incompatible with the personal vision beginning to take deep root in his mind and heart.

Within a few years Darrow courageously abandoned his comfortable position of affluence. He quit his job defending the railroad. His new clients came from the huge underclass. The labor leaders struggling for the right to organize became his new clients; teachers became his clients; mental patients became his clients. Darrow fought for the disenfranchised, even though they often could not pay his fee. Darrow took on not only the cases but also the *causes* of individuals without political influence. He became the populist champion of every man, woman, and child who he believed had been trampled under by the heavy feet of corrupt industry and government. Darrow's new mission did not pay well, nor did it grant him the possibility of becoming an influential power broker within America's "Established Bar."

Darrow, with conviction and determination and a willingness to sacrifice ordinary rewards in order to reach a high ground of service, was fashioning for himself a "right livelihood." His career choices returned him work that allowed his head to connect with his heart, and his heart to connect with his words and deeds. He recognized that lawyering could fit his criteria for right livelihood. All that was required was that he make adjustments to how he lawyered along the way.

Todd Alley has practiced law for almost twenty years. He, too, has made adjustments along the way:

> *I fired a client several years ago because what she expected of me was inconsistent with what I expect of myself. I had far too long convinced myself that my training and my*

*professional responsibility created a world of grey area where the rules were different from those I sought to follow raising my children, or interacting with my spouse, or in company with my friends.*

*I had convinced myself that this grey world was confined within the four walls of my law office, but during the representation of this client, I felt that greyness expanding farther and farther beyond those four walls.*

*There were a thousand ways I could find to ethically justify what I was being asked to do. I had, by way of convoluted mental gymnastics, convinced myself that my professional obligations required me to serve this client—mean spirit or not. The easy next step became an obsession with winning at all costs.*

*Then I experienced a real kind of breakthrough in understanding. It was unusually liberating when I recognized that I was serving my own selfish financial needs, that what I had been seeing as my client's greed was in part my own greed.*

## YOU WON'T FIND IT "IN THE BOOKS"

The way to right livelihood in lawyering does not begin with a lawyer-like understanding of the Code of Professional Responsibility. EC 7-8, for example, does not provide us with mystical insight into wrong or right conduct in lawyering. It may help us "justify" our wrong conduct, in fact, as easily as it guides us to right conduct. It certainly fails to help us gain any real insight into what our heart should be telling our head or what our head should be telling our hands.

Such ethical codes are created in the process of our best attempts as lawyers to put down on paper what is arguably acceptable or arguably unacceptable, what is *probably* right conduct or what is *probably* wrong conduct, what is just and what is unjust. Codes of ethical resposibility at least provide us with some means and motivation for keeping to the high ground in our day-to-day lawyering. But they are not the last word. The "last word" rests with each lawyer.

Finding peace with tough decisions in lawyering becomes much easier when we constantly remind ourselves that, first, we are members in equal standing within the broader community of mankind; and, second, we are professionals within a much narrower community of lawyers, and that the two worlds are inextricably linked together.

There is not a line of demarcation that separates one from the other so that we move into one and out of the other as we drive from our home to our office in the morning, and from our office to our home in the evening. The truths that we choose to govern our lives at home as we interact with our children and our spouses may just as easily be shared and explained to our clients, our partners, and our peers.

The prophets Amos and Micah preached a simple message to the Israelites in an effort to spare their people from suffering. Their Old Testament writings said again and again that the laws of men tell mankind very little about what is spiritually right, just, or honest. They preached that the Pharisees distorted the concepts of right and wrong by paying attention to form and ceremony over the substance and the heart of spirituality. The verbose, detailed, tedious commentary and analysis by the Pharisees had tarnished the beautiful simplicity of enlightened living. They tried to make the "heart" of the matter into rules for the "head." In the process, concepts of justice, honesty, and "right and wrong" became muddled and unfocused. There is a Yiddish parable that well illustrates what Amos and Micah wanted their people to understand:

*Rabbi Hillel was approached by a rabbinical student who asked if the Rabbi could teach him all there is to know about Judaism while the student stood on one leg. Rabbi Hillel burst into a fit of anger and accused the young student of shamefully mocking all that is sacred about the teachings of Judaism by asking such a foolish question.*

*The student then approached Rabbi Akiba and asked the Rabbi whether he could teach him all there is to know about Judaism while the student stood on one leg. Rabbi Akiba wisely pondered the student's question for what seemed to be an eternity for the student. Finally, Rabbi Akiba told the student to stand on one leg. As the student stood in front of the Rabbi, the Rabbi spoke these words: "Do justice. Do no harm to anyone, and treat all people the same way you wish to be treated. The rest of what you need to learn is all commentary."*

Rabbi Akiba demonstrated the greater wisdom of the two rabbis because he recognized that there are some principles for living that do not require intricate analysis and codification. In fact, it is almost always the case that something important gets lost when we attempt to "wordsmith wisdom." Our own professional codes of conduct do not simply or clearly state what we know in our hearts at every moment to be the right course of action.

## First the chicken, then the egg?

Huston Smith said, "If we take the world's religions at their best, we discover the distilled wisdom of the human spirit."

Smith has studied religious wisdom for more than sixty years. He has journeyed to Mecca, participated in Passover feasts, practiced *zazen* side by side with Buddhist monks, and received Holy Communion in his own Methodist church. He has been on a journey of spiritual discovery his entire adult life. Theological historians will mark well what Huston Smith brought home to the rest of us as a result of his journey.

One belief that he is able to share with us is that mankind was able to create laws, the ones that are the foundation of our livelihoods as lawyers, about how to live, because we have an inherent understanding of justice and injustice. We have an inherent understanding of honesty and dishonesty, right and wrong. It is this inherent understanding that was written on our hearts before language could create statutory versions of laws to live by.

## Leadership requires courage

Lawyering becomes and remains an exemplary right livelihood when we consistently lead our clients, our partners, and our peers to a "better place." Clients or partners cannot compel lawyers to shred documents or misrepresent the truth in the discovery process. The lawyer alone is responsible. It is the lawyer and none other who ultimately turns on the document shredder or signs his name to discovery pleadings that don't really represent the truth.

It is the lawyer alone who fails to tell a client or partner: "This is the way I work. This is what I will do. This is what I won't do." Complying with what the lawyer's conscience tells her to do is as easy as telling the client or the partner "no." Will someone else sign the pleading that we refuse to sign? Absolutely. Does that fact somehow diminish or negate the importance of this choice that we have made for ourselves? Absolutely not.

Darrow's way of saying no to the type of lawyering he did not like was to change jobs, taking a big cut in pay and prestige. He went from being a well-paid railroad defense lawyer to a woefully underpaid civil rights and criminal defense lawyer. But in the switch he established consistency and continuity between what his hands did and what his head and heart told him to do—thought, word, and deed were in sync. In doing what is almost unimaginable for the typical lawyer of the '90s, he showed incredible courage that still props up his name as a great lawyer almost six decades after his death in 1938. In Darrow's mind, some money just costs too much.

Clarence Darrow, from his often fatalistic, cynical point of view, might have criticized Micah and Amos for trying to oversimplify a chaotic and complex world. In attitude and practice, however, Darrow's view of the world was similarly a matter of a few simple truths about human behavior. Those truths became the fulcrum upon which he sought to find balance in the way he conducted himself as a lawyer. He did not need ECs or DRs from the Code of Professional Responsibility to tell him when his lawyering world was out of balance. The obvious did not escape him. If it had a big beak, feathers, and two webbed feet, and it made a "quacking" sound, he recognized that it was a duck (or one of its cousins).

There is an interesting passage in Kevin Tierney's *Darrow, A Biography* where Tierney describes Darrow as an agnostic on the one hand and a religious scholar on the other:

> *His Bible was as well thumbed as any preacher's; even his anti-religion fed upon a curiosity and thirst for explanation of a peculiarly religious character. Like George Bernard Shaw, he gave biblical study as much priority as a preacher.*

With all his study of the Bible, still Darrow never sought or claimed a conversion to Christianity, but he applied the wisdom it offered every day in the way he lived as a lawyer. He conducted his life without religious ceremony of any kind. Darrow preferred to figure out by himself and for himself what type of wisdom would govern his life. If that wisdom frequently coincided with, say, what Jesus taught, still that did not motivate him to stop his own personal study and become a Christian. For most of us lawyers who are practitioners of a declared faith, going it alone would seem difficult, and, at any rate, not necessary.

## GOING WHERE SEVERAL HAVE GONE

Five times a day, the devout Muslim kneels down facing east and prays to Allah. The frequent repetition helps him reaffirm his beliefs and keep them almost always in the front of his mind. For the devout Muslim, the prayer ritual helps him avoid becoming too long separated from his spiritual life as he goes about his business life; the two areas of his life are inseparably intertwined. His spiritual life is likewise interconnected in varying degrees with all the subparts of his life. His prayers five times a day remind him of that.

The Christian goes through the same process in his church on Sundays. All religions similarly emphasize a time and a place for a ceremony of reaffirmation. The ritual is important to remind the believer of his beliefs.

Maintaining the principle of right livelihood in lawyering sometimes requires such a ceremonial "reality check" at the mosque, the temple, or the synagogue, or in the confessional at the cathedral. It is in these places that we are able to remind ourselves that we live according to truths and by principles that are not for sale. These places help us to remember our core values, and that we cannot compromise or otherwise distort those values in our interactions with clients, partners, and peers.

Clarence Darrow rejected the notion that he needed the "North Star" held out for guidance by religious faith. His declared cynicism would not permit such backsliding. Most of us, however, aren't under the burden of living up to a cynic's creed. We are free to take advantage of anything out there that can help us make lawyering a right livelihood.

**"**

*It matters not how many small ambitions*
*we may seem to have achieved. . . .*
*All triumphs are futile*
*without the victory over self;*
*and when the triumph over self is won,*
*there are no more battles to be fought,*
*for all the world is then at peace.*
                                    *—Clarence Darrow*

## PART THREE

### THE EGO

Clarence Darrow lived through a long stretch of years, even by today's actuarial tables for men. He died in Chicago in 1938 at the age of eighty-one. While I am not writing a biography of the great lawyer, there are some things about his "history" that bear saying.

It was on a frosty April night in 1857 near the small town of Kinsman, Ohio, that Emily Darrow gave birth to her fifth child, her third son. Either she or Amirus, the boy's father, named him Clarence Seward without giving a moment's thought to whether that was a name befitting someone who would become the most celebrated lawyer in America. "The one satisfaction I have had in connection with this cross," said Darrow of his given name, "was that the boys never could think up any nickname half so inane as the real one my parents adorned me with."

Nevertheless, Darrow made a name for himself with the name he did not love. The showbiz newspaper *Variety* described him as "America's greatest one-man stage draw." It is true that his legendary performances in the 1920s as defense attorney in the Scopes "monkey trial" and the Leopold-Loeb "thrill-killing" case made him a hot property, both in and out of Hollywood. His courtroom brilliance inspired the movie *Inherit the Wind,* and Henry Fonda saw fit to develop a one-man act based on his career. Darrow has been called the "most celebrated American lawyer of the twentieth century." But it is what Clarence Darrow fought so hard to become and not the screen or stage that guarantees the continuing prominence of his name among the great characters in American life and history.

He had little formal education, briefly attending Allegheny College and the University of Michigan, but was admitted to the Ohio Bar before he turned twenty-two. He was a fiercely independent young man. His self-reliant determination often set him against "joint-stock" causes and positions. His reputation was built by lawyering for men despised and even vilified in living rooms and at kitchen tables across the nation. Nevertheless, he was a larger-than-life folk hero and populist prophet.

## CLARENCE DARROW, THE JOURNEYMAN

Darrow was always in a state of "becoming," of growing continuously toward insight and wisdom. His process of becoming carried him through a stage of self-centered, ego-driven vanity toward what could best be described as enlightened wisdom toward the end of his life. Between those two extremes lie the lessons left behind by Darrow.

The road map to wisdom left by Darrow has a moderate amount of detail that is most accurate and honest, I believe, when spoken by himself and not biographers and historians. As lawyers, we will be able to identify intellectually if not experientially with the critical turns in the road for Darrow, the dead ends, the seemingly interminable distances from "here to there." Our career choice has at least placed us on the same road with him, although we are certainly in the driver's seat and may choose the way and the speed at which we travel. We may, however, even choose to get home by an entirely different road.

## THE EGO IS WHERE WE BEGIN

Each of us is probably at a different stage of personal transformation, depending on how long we have been practicing law. Some of us have already covered one or several of the same stretches of ground as Darrow. Wherever we are, most of us began the trek from the same place, taking our fuel from the same station and pump: superpremium *93-octane ego.*

Only a few of us can answer honestly that we entered the business of lawyering for predominantly humanitarian reasons. More than we would like to admit, it was our egos that drove our career choice, not our altruism. David Halberg's objective honesty helps explore this topic a little closer:

> *I always feel like I am in a beauty contest when some well-meaning friend or acquaintance asks me why I became a lawyer. I visualize the contestant telling the judge that she should be Miss Idaho because she is the contestant who is best able to "change the world" or "make a difference." In fact, what she is really thinking is that if she is chosen as Miss Idaho, she wins big prizes. The folks back home revere her name and she then may go on to be Miss America. Her ego drove her to the contest to begin with and it is her ego that will be fed if she wins. That is how it is for many of us as lawyers. Our ego gave us a ride to the contest, and it drives us to and from our offices every day.*

A "healthy ego" that fuels confidence in our ability to do just about anything is a highly volatile thing that can easily mutate into destructive self-centeredness. That is when ego has become *amour-propre*, self-love that distinguishes and sets "me" apart from less fortunate "others." An inflated ego is full of hot, explosive air that often is an extremely pernicious force in our professional and personal lives. Clarence Darrow said that he thought the battle against ego was a lifetime struggle:

> *All human egos place prime importance upon themselves; each is the center of the great circle around which all else revolves; no one can see or feel in any other way. Although all intelligent people realize that they are as nothing in the procession that is ever moving on, yet we cannot but feel that when we are dead the parade will no longer move.*

Wayne Alford is a trial lawyer who describes the struggle this way:

> *Early on, young trial lawyers are wrestling with their ego. We want enough ego on hand to bolster our self-confidence when we walk into a courtroom those first times. We need*

*enough ego to reinforce our belief in the integrity and correctness of our decisions, the validity of our advice. And trying to guarantee enough ego sometimes leads to the development of considerably more than enough ego.*

*This is when it has become imperative that we, like the tortoise, lose the old shell and exchange ego and fear for something more genuinely secure. Most truly great lawyers inevitably exchange an overused sense of self-importance for understated substance of character. The lawyers in our ranks who are unable to make such a transition pass through their careers and their lives held captive in a world that evolves only around themselves. Sometimes, their financial success blinds them to the fact that, intellectually, spiritually, and emotionally, they remain crippled by their self-centeredness.*

Buddhists believe that *tanha,* or the self-controlling ego, is the cause of man's greatest suffering and that selfish craving is the root of human misery. More importantly, their belief is that it is difficult to advance toward any significant degree of wisdom until the struggle with the ego has been put in check. Perhaps the world's Buddhists are wrong in the way they analyze this topic; however, their belief should at least motivate most of those in our ranks to listen and look more closely.

The Apostle Paul, when establishing a new church there, wrote a letter to the converts at Philippi counseling them that ego and the pride and the self-centeredness it fostered were destructive to each person and to the whole group. Paul knew that the mind's eye is blinded by an overblown and illusory sense of self-importance:

> *Don't be selfish; don't live to make a good impression on others. Be humble, thinking of others as better than yourself. Don't think only about your own affairs, but be interested in others, too, and what they are doing.*

Even at trial, while fulfilling a duty to your client, it is unhealthy to nurture preoccupations with how you are distinguished from the rest of the community of "less fortunate others." Usually, the distinction the ego would have us make is that we are the reverse of what Paul advised the Philippians, that we are better persons than the opponent we face. Such a misguided notion is at odds with sound thinking and good judgment.

The ego that perhaps served us well by boosting our fledgling confidence when we first began to feel our way along the road as lawyers can hinder our entire journey if we do not keep it at a manageable level. It hinders our journey by making us believe too much in ourselves and not putting enough stock in other people and what they have to say, their ideas, their beliefs and notions. We miss out on what the world around us has to offer.

Clarence Darrow was able to admit—to the consternation of his ego, no doubt—that an autobiography is never entirely true. "No one can get the right perspective on himself." But I believe his perspective was right, and universally true, when he declared, "I am interested not in the way that I have fashioned the world, but in the way the world has molded me."

By this statement Darrow acknowledges that he is not at the center of his universe and that his universe or even his community does not revolve around him. He therefore makes the first step toward putting his sense of self-importance in perspective. Darrow said it was "doubtless a certain vanity" that moved him to write about himself, but he also said he knew that neither he "nor any one else has the slightest importance in time and space." It is clear that Darrow thought about the folly and tragedy of an unhealthy ego.

Most biographers point out that in Darrow's early career as a fledgling lawyer he was driven by pure ego. He was obsessed with a need for recognition. Kevin Tierney, perhaps one of Darrow's most insightful biographers, describes Darrow's early years as constant labor to have his community listen to *his* words, recognize *his* insights, admire *his* talent and ability, and seek out *his* services as a great lawyer. Tierney, in his biography *Darrow*, said of Darrow's early years as a lawyer in Chicago:

> *Nowhere else was competition among young hopefuls so intense as in Chicago; they flocked from every part of the nation to capture the city's prizes. It was no place for the reticent. Looking about him, Darrow felt an overwhelming need to make up for lost time . . . impatient to embrace the golden future that was rightfully his. In his effort to gain recognition, he became pushy, struggling to the front of the crowd to shake the hand of some notable, or writing out of the blue to the famous."*

In their early years of lawyering, most lawyers impatiently push themselves to the front of the crowd. They believe that in a crowd it is only the first few rows of people who lead, who speak for the rest of the crowd, who sometimes gain the admiration of the rest. Most young lawyers, just like Darrow, believe with every ounce of their conviction that they are the one "best suited" to stand in the front row of any crowd. It is similar to the mindset we see in some politicians, particularly the young ones or those just beginning a political career. A tremendous amount of arrogance is embedded in the belief that moves one of our fellow citizens to think that he or she is ideally equipped to lead you and me, and make decisions for the rest of the community. Does that politician actually recognize a clearer and better path for us that we fail to grasp? Or is that politician simply moving to the first few rows of the crowd to assuage his self-image needs?

Darrow's ego, however strong in his early lawyering career, was not allowed to become destructive or aberrational. It was probably healthy at that stage in his career, since he found himself in a setting that was consistently confrontational. Confrontation drives ego, and in return the ego assures us that we have the "stuff" to win the good fight. The young lawyer's path to survival, to what he sees as his best chance for success and recognition, requires taking a place at the front of the crowd. However, the ego will gladly lead—and drag you along for the next thirty years if you are not very careful.

## EGO AS THE WEAPON OF CHOICE

When two contestants rattle sabers at each other, each may truly believe he is better armed than his opponent, with superior strength, skill, and strategy. Each believes totally that he will prevail. Ego drives that belief, and also rushes in to fill any momentary doubts that may arise. Every lawyer's image of himself is of the victor, taking home the spoils of war. The image has come down to him, strong and clear, from generations of lawyers before him who have engaged in similar battles.

Wholesale belief in this valiant image, however, almost surely puts the young lawyer into jeopardy. It is not unlike trying overzealously to conform to parental expectations—which, in themselves, are ego-drenched—while ignoring inner guidance to advance with caution.

Unfortunately, our early years as lawyers are typically not kinder and gentler years and do not afford us many opportunities to lay aside our egos. The survival mode kicks in right away. And these are truly formative years in a lawyering life; lessons bought hard during this time are not easily discarded in favor of "nobler" attitudes.

Archie Lamb, an experienced and very talented trial lawyer from Birmingham, Alabama, reflected upon his very early years with these insights:

> *Throughout my first few years of practice, I assembled what I often refer to as my "bag of tricks." In my mind's eye it looks like a dentist's bag and is filled with all the tools I have used to extract any and everything I needed from all with whom I interacted professionally. There are tools for manipulation, subtle or direct; tools for posturing; gamesmanship tools, well-honed and lethal.*

> *My bag of tricks was heavy with ego. It was weighted down by pride and self-centered motives. I can see that now. But in the early years, I relied on my bag of tricks, clung to*

> *it in the belief it made me a better, more capable lawyer. It was my surest means for protecting number one. In truth, and in retrospect, I only began to really grow as a lawyer when I set my bag of tricks aside, relying less on ego and more on something deeper with more substance. Wisdom? Maybe. What is certain is the difference in the better way I feel, unburdened by my bag of tricks.*

The danger of the ego years lies in the failure to recognize the wisdom of moving on, or perhaps the inability to move beyond the seeming comfort and security of those years. For many the cement has hardened too completely, and for them the mold is permanently set. "After all," one might say, "that bag of tricks served me well in my early years of lawyering. Why tinker with a thing that works?"

The Upanishads, sacred Hindu literature, teach that spiritual advancement is marked by a mind, heart, and spirit that becomes increasingly vibrant and powerful, yet peaceful and serene, while the body, on the other hand, is beginning to wrinkle and sag with age. The faithful Hindu does not concern himself with the lines of age that show in his aging face, but takes great joy from his developing spirit. Unhealthy ego focuses our concern on just the opposite.

The image preservation Kim Evers spoke of earlier on in the book is the thing that drives us not only to "keep up with the Joneses" but to far exceed them and run over them in the process if we must. It is what keeps us from having a meaningful friendship with them, or even caring much about how they feel or what great thoughts and ideas they might have. It leads us to the point where we are willing to manipulate the Joneses at the drop of a hat if such manipulation will further our material gain or increase our fame, power, and influence. It causes us to be suspicious and downright paranoid about what they might be up to. It helps us to forget that the Joneses are citizens of that community that Sol Linowitz says we should serve. It becomes impossible to serve anyone or anything but yourself when you permit an unhealthy ego to lead you around in this world.

## LEAVING EGO IN THE REARVIEW MIRROR

The ego years should serve only as a transitional step to get us over our inexperience, and beyond our sense of insecurity. Our professional public image has suffered, in part, from a *minority* in our ranks who seem suspended in time, trapped and held prisoner by a sticky web of image preservation. These are unable to enjoy a transformation capable of carrying us beyond unhealthy ego. They have beaten back natural desires to grow and develop toward greater self-realization and away from intense self-interest. Status and possessions hold their field of vision at or below the horizon, when what lies over the horizon exceeds anything they have known so far. Darrow believed that we must never stop growing and learning, that we must move on, that continuous transformation is essential:

*Life is a never-ending school, and the really important lessons all tend to teach man his proper relation to the environment where he must live. With wild ambitions and desires untamed, we are spawned onto a shoreless sea ... no lights nor headlands stand to point the proper way the voyager should take, he is left to sail an untried bark across an angry sea.*

Darrow took risks and ventured far, but not at the mercy of "wild ambitions and desires untamed." He had ambition and desire, but they did not have him. He never lost touch with his guiding conscience. We are faced with the same decisions about our journey ahead. If we stay too close inside the harbor line of our habitual way of thinking, we are left where we started. We are stuck with our limited bag of tricks, and are preserving an image of lawyers and lawyering that, quite frankly, the Joneses have grown intolerant and tired of.

**"**

*It takes long effort and training
to make any real progress
in teaching kindness and mutual help.
These qualities come from
the development of imagination,
which is of slow growth.*
— *Clarence Darrow*

# PART FOUR

## THE JOURNEYMAN

Real progress in learning begins when we start recognizing that people and ideas are important and interesting even when they don't agree with us, even when they don't serve our selfish and narrow need to be bigger and better.

The first stage beyond an unhealthy, overlarge ego is the Journeyman stage. Our sense of purpose and direction begins to take the first tentative steps away from "me first," with an increasing emphasis on and concern for how our behavior impacts others. The Journeyman also has a heightened interest in broadening and deepening his awareness of the great world of ideas. He is determined to grow in his understanding of those ideas.

After Darrow confronted William Jennings Bryan in the Scopes trial, he offered some observations about what made Bryan so vulnerable as a lawyer. He described Bryan as a man frozen in time, a man who had ceased to grow intellectually: "His speculations had ripened into unchangeable convictions. He did not *think*. He *knew*." (Italics added.)

Darrow further describes Bryan as a man who was the antithesis of the Journeyman, suggesting that Bryan's personal journey might have ended at the ego stage of lawyering. And such is the case too often for many others in our ranks—we don't think, we know. We have, after all, completed nineteen years of school. Darrow said this:

> *Few people try to think. Most of them deliberately chloroform themselves lest a random*

*thought might find lodgement in their brains. But with cocksureness, they glibly advise others how to live and what to do.*

In Kevin Tierney's Darrow biography, he describes Darrow as a man in search of knowledge, knowledge on a broad range of subjects and topics, all of which would become the grist for wisdom's mill.

*He was a popularizer whose intellectual disposition was immediately related to the world around him, and who became one of the best-read men of his time. Not only because of the quantity of books he had consumed, but also because of his capacity to retain their ideas.*

Ideas are the stuff of wisdom and enlightened living. However, you cannot merely commit an idea to memory like learning the Pledge of Allegiance and hope to have it serve you when you need it. Darrow knew that one must understand an idea from inside one's own realm of experience and insight in order to employ the idea. The capacity for *application* of important ideas is a necessary predicate to functional wisdom.

## THINKING LIKE A LAWYER

In time many of us discover that the intellectual and philosophical requirements of lawyering are contrary to notions we might have had in law school. Martin Levin has practiced law for nine years. He sees it this way:

> *It took nine years of practicing law for me to realize that there is not much requirement for philosophical thinking in lawyering. The way to think as a lawyer has been handed down to me from preceding generations of lawyers. Most of us are kidding ourselves if we believe that we own any high ground in the world of wisdom just because we have been trained as lawyers and can think like a lawyer. My observations lead me to believe that we have narrowed and refined what we think about until we all think alike, to the detriment of the people we serve.*

*If there existed a school designed to train ad-
venturers or explorers to think like lawyers,
the continent of North America would still
be a fanciful legend.*

## STAYING AWAKE

Clarence Darrow showed an untiring commitment to think. He continuously rejected the
tendency to "think like a lawyer." He struggled
to illuminate and broaden what he knew about
himself and the people he served.

*As one journeys along, he gains experiences
and even some ideas. Accumulated opinions
and philosophy may be more important to
others than the bare facts about how he lived,
so my ambition is not so much to relate the
occurrences as to record the ideas that life
has forced me to accept; after all, thoughts,
impressions, and feelings are really life itself.*

Darrow understood that mastering his trade required that he not allow his feelings to atrophy.
He was not willing to accept the "impressions

and feelings" of others about how he should live and lawyer. Instead, listening to his own deepest convictions told him more about lawyering than he could possibly learn in a law book. "Impressions and feelings" really did make up "life itself" for Darrow in and out of lawyering. They helped point him toward enlightened living.

There are some striking similarities in what the Koran, the Bible, and the Talmud have to say about enlightenment. They all suggest that their brand of enlightenment—even if dressed differently—begins with awakening.

> *Buddha was asked: "Are you a God?"*
> *"No," he said.*
> *"Are you a Prophet?"*
> *"No."*
> *"Are you a Saint?"*
> *"No."*
> *"Then what are you?"*
> *"I am awake."*

Darrow was awake. Impressions and feelings kept him awake. The business of lawyering most of the time is scary enough to help us keep our eyes wide open. Calculating profit margins sometimes keeps us right at the edge of "frenzy." The only "impressions and feelings" we are aware of in such a mode are the ones that remind us to bring in more business, meet more deadlines, and figure out ways to be bigger and better. We certainly cannot afford to be asleep as we maneuver through our world of high-stakes business.

In that mode, with our eyes fixed and wide open, we are still not awake by Darrow's standards. It is as if we were traveling on a bus with all the shades pulled down. Most of the trip we spend squabbling with each other about who deserves the better seats. We occupy our minds so fully with strategies for jockeying for a better seat, that it rarely occurs to us to let up a shade and look out the window. Not only are landscapes and scenery rushing past unappreciated, but often we are not sure where the bus is going, or why it is traveling in a particular direction, or what to expect when we get there. Putting our "nose to the grindstone" can keep our necks bent and keep us looking down most of our lives. Darrow had the stamina to work extremely hard as an attorney. If a trial required twenty hours a day, he would work twenty hours a day. Darrow deplored work for work's sake, however. He rejected a work regimen that left no room for living. Writing in *The Story of My Life*, Darrow said:

> *In Europe, no one is afraid to enjoy life in his own way. There the people have never heard of Benjamin Franklin and his tribe. Here we have been taught that "early to bed and early to rise, makes a man healthy, wealthy, and wise." Neither does Europe seem to have imbibed Henry Ford's idea of efficiency. I saw no working men sitting alongside a moving platform with their eyes staring ahead to note when a nut or a screw or a spoke or a rod would pass their way. These neither went to bed early nor began to work early.*

Clarence Darrow was a contemporary of Sinclair Lewis and, like Lewis, was convinced that the Puritan work ethic drained imagination, creativity, and potential for personal growth. He believed that experiences, his reflection, and his focused thinking should not only elevate his horizons as a lawyer but leave him time to enjoy the landscape, time to stay awake.

The idea that awakening precedes enlightenment is an idea that has been "discovered" and rediscovered, illustrated and reillustrated by thinkers and philosophers for centuries. In 1945, Charles P. Curtis Jr. co-authored *The Practical Cogitator: The Thinker's Anthology*. Curtis practiced law in Boston for thirty-five years. During that time, he taught constitutional law at Harvard and was able to write books on topics ranging from lion hunting to world economics. Curtis was very much awake.

*The Practical Cogitator* is described as "a one-volume book that represents the wisdom of the ages." The editors called the book "a sort of 'cerebral coast pilot,' a compilation of essential passages on the great themes of life." There is a passage in the book that borrows a modernized, modified, version of Plato's concept of awakening. The theme is borrowed from *The Cave,* written by Plato around 330 B.C.

*Suppose a race of men who were born and brought up all their lives in a movie, who have never taken their eyes off the screen. All they have ever seen are the pictures, and all they have ever heard, except each other, is the sound track. That, and only that, is their world.*

*I am not concerned with what sort of picture they see. My point is that all they see, all they have ever seen, are pictures on a screen; and that those pictures are all the reality they know.*

*Now suppose that one of them is taken out; forcibly, because he is being taken away from everything he has been used to, from everything he regards as his world and his life. He is taken out into the sunlight, and the sunlight blinds him. The glitter and dazzle hurt him, and he cannot see any of the things he is shown, the things we now tell him are real. He would have to get slowly used to these real things perhaps by looking sideways at them at first, or at their shadows, or by looking at the stars or at the moon, before he could look at things by the light of the sun, let alone the sun itself.*

*What would he think, when he was finally able to look at these real things? He would know at last that it is the sun that relates the seasons and the courses of time, and that the sun is the reason behind all that he and his comrades used to see on the screen.*

Darrow spent most of his life moving farther into the sunlight. He typically rejected the view of reality that was handed down to him by those who went before him. Darrow woke up to his own notion about what is real, and what is important.

## AFTER AWAKENING . . . WHAT THEN?

After awakening comes the hard part—transformation. The transformation this chapter discusses is one where we move away from all the time "thinking like a lawyer" to thinking like a Journeyman. The Journeyman is a different kind of hunter and gatherer from the typical lawyer. The Darrow-like Journeyman is committed to gathering new ideas, notions, impressions, inspirations, substance, images, and wisdom that help him not to think exclusively "like a lawyer."

The type of wisdom the Darrow-like journeyman is after cannot be found by holing up in a law office and working twelve-hour days doing only lawyer work. It cannot be found by the attorney whose entire identity is single-dimensional. The man or woman whose only identity is "attorney" will have a more difficult time beginning a search for the type of wisdom or enlightenment Darrow was after. It will be harder for this person to move into the sunlight. The single-dimensional attorney does not see a relationship between wisdom and material gain, or enlightenment and power, or insight and influence, so why bother? If it cannot be owned, possessed, bought or sold, how does it improve my life as a lawyer?

Clarence Darrow believed that ideas, notions, inspirations, images, experience, memories, knowledge, and generally paying attention to life beyond the "bottom line" made him a better lawyer and a better human being. What he borrowed from the world of ideas, philosophy, science, and theology, for example, was put to good use with clients, judges, juries, and opposing counsel. As an advocate, negotiator, and counselor he was able to show them more than a one-dimensional identity.

So, where do we find all this stuff that Darrow believed was so important?

## PAY ATTENTION TO WHAT WE KNOW

Most transformations are a process of rebirth, or reillumination, a process of simply *remembering* truths and realities rather than discovering new ones. "How to live" writers have built an industry around trying to make us remember what we have been told all of our lives about living wisely. "Improved living" peddlers have tried to spoon-feed the American public with thirty-second sound bites designed to help us remember "what our parents taught us," or "what we learned in kindergarten." Calendars, video tapes, posters, and fifty-page keepsake books promise to jumpstart our heart, mind, spirit, and soul—restating what we already know. New Age writers have taken the virtues industry to a new level of commercial success by suggesting that the world is really more mystical and mysterious than we ever suspected.

New Age gurus tell us that they have discovered "insights" that have somehow been dormant and unrevealed for centuries. They suggest that we should leap to a "new plane of understanding." New Age writers speak of new realities, new truths, "new and improved" rules for living. However, when most of these "new insights" are placed side by side with old truths and insights, it is difficult to make much of a distinction. The ideas, images, inspirations, truths, notions, values and wisdom offered by these easy-to-read "how to live" books merely restate and reaffirm what we at one time have already learned. Most of the fundamentals about wise and enlightened living have been known to us at least from  the time we were first given a license to drive a car.

## YOU CARRY IT WITH YOU

If you were to take a pencil and a piece of paper and jot down all the wisdom you have carried around in your head and heart since you were a teenager, you would discover something remarkable. The Beatitudes, Solomon's Proverbs, ideas about the Eightfold Path, ideas from the Upanishads, ideas from the Koran, and Confucius's Doctrine of the Mean would all appear on your paper in one form or another. You would also recognize classic philosophical themes found in great literature written by Shakespeare, Steinbeck, Conrad, Buck, etc., etc.

The difference between Darrow as a Journeyman and many of us who lawyer with a single-dimensional identity is that Darrow was willing to constantly struggle to better understand, substantially expand and fully integrate into his life the ideas that appeared on "his piece of paper." Many of us, on the other hand, are willing to move from fiscal year to fiscal year, from acquisition to acquisition, from bottom line to bottom line, thinking only about things that we can pigeon-hole into that single-dimensional space that we mistakenly believe is "living and lawyering" to the fullest. Much of what we already know about wiser living we do not regularly expand upon or fully integrate into our lives because it does not seem relevant to the task at hand, staying in business.

Distant echoes of what we have learned about wiser living in the course of our lives remain just that, distant echoes, because the clamor or din attibuted to becoming bigger and better is overpoweringly loud. Once we have taken inventory of all the "wise" things we already know, where else do we look for ways to enlighten our lives? How can we increase the number of our dimensions from one to many?

## LISTENING TO FELLOW-TRAVELERS

Most of the rules to live by that are suggested in the book of Proverbs are not the thoughts of an intellectual elite. Proverbs is a compilation of ideas about how to improve quality of life that were handed down from generations of laborers, servants, scribes, teachers, kings, and generally people from almost every walk of life. Christianity and Buddhism were not built around writings by Jesus or Buddha.

In fact, neither teacher wrote the first word about his lessons for living but instead relied on fishermen, laborers, servants, physicians, teachers, tentmakers—all forms and fashions of people who heard, interpreted, and delivered their messages. These messengers came from all walks of life—from servants to kings. Each not only spread the word about the ideas he heard, but also improved and expanded upon the message. Buddha and Jesus must have believed that everyone had something important to offer, that the value of everyone's ideas should at least be heard and considered.

After many years of lawyering, some of us begin believing that anything more than we already know is superfluous. We know how to generate business because we *need* to know. Our friends and neighbors, the mechanic who works on our car, the carpenter who works on our home, the waiter who serves us cannot help us with our type of need-to-know information.

How to pay bills and how to keep our law practice flourishing cannot be improved upon by the advice of people from just any walk of life. However, need-to-know information is only that one-dimensional stuff we have been discussing in the foregoing paragraphs of this chapter. When all we think about is the business of lawyering, we miss out on ideas that can make us wiser. We stop listening to family, friends, neighbors, and "ordinary" people. We lose interest in them because they do not fit into our one-dimensional world. We often pay minimal attention to them because we view them as a distraction within our tightly wound, tightly focused world of lawyering. Darrow shed light on the issue this way:

> *When we abandon the thought of immortality we at least have cast out fear. We gain a certain dignity and self-respect. We regard*

*our fellow-travelers as companions in the pleasures and tribulations of life. We feel an interest in them, knowing that we are all moved by common impulses and touched by mutual understanding. We gain kinship with the world.*

Many lawyers within our ranks will never know the "kinship" Darrow was trying to describe. As a result, they will never learn the wisdom of those "fellow-travelers" and "companions" whom Darrow so dearly loved. Darrow was not bogged down by a sense of elitism or arrogance about the space he occupied in this world. He was willing to listen to the wisdom offered by everyone. He heard, noticed, and learned more about people because few people were "unimportant" or uninteresting to him. Here is a passage from *Clarence Darrow for the Defense* that explores that quality:

*He had a kind word for everyone and took time to talk to each, inquiring into their daily life, thereby making them feel that he was an old and very dear friend. A man from Ohio says, "Darrow was scheduled to make a Labor Day speech at Akron. My friend and I decided to make a pilgrimage from Cleveland to hear that speech. After the meeting we walked over to the hotel, and there was Darrow, standing in the lobby talking to another man. My friend, who was a complete stranger to him, dragged me over to Darrow. He accepted our introductions as a matter of course. It wasn't long before the four of us were lined up at the hotel bar having a drink. Then we sat down to a table in the dining room for a thirty-five-cent dinner, Dutch treat."*

## WANT TO KNOW VS. NEED TO KNOW

Buddhists have a confounding saying: "If you meet Buddha on the road, kill him." Why would adherents to the Buddhist faith advise their followers to kill their great Teacher? So that the shock of the statement will alert you to the importance of its message. What is meant by the saying is that Buddha's ideas about enlightened living had no meaning without inner work on the part of those who hear his message. Better Buddha were not even on hand to teach than for followers to merely parrot his sayings. Any ideas about better living that Buddha had to offer were powerless unless those ideas were meshed with what most people already know. The ideas then needed to be critically analyzed, clearly focused, and, most important, forever remembered. People hearing Buddha's words needed a *want*, a real desire to understand how those words could improve their lives.

In law school, using the Socratic method for getting from Point A to Point B was usually agonizing, especially when the instructor pointing the way from A to B inadequately understood and misapplied the ancient learning tool. Prepackaged outlines prepared by professionals such as Mister Emanuel and Mister Gilbert spoke to us much more clearly. They got us to Point B without convoluted analysis. They took us there quickly when many instructors simply did not have the talent or ability to do the same.

There is no prepackaged outline, however, that we may use to lead us from Point A to Point B, if we describe Point A as *awakening* and Point

B as the first step beyond it. There are no quick and easy steps for wiser, more enlightened living—not for intelligent lawyers, and not for reverent Buddhist monks.

Darrow was critical of people's unwillingness to think, to form ideas of their own. He fought against a narrow vision of life and experiences that prevented the fullest measure of understanding what motivates human conduct.

> *Very few schools encourage the young or the old to think out questions for themselves. And yet life is a continuous problem . . . and first of all we should be equipped to think, if possible.*

There is a story about a young man who approached Socrates and begged to become his pupil so that he might acquire wisdom. Socrates had the young man follow him to the shores of a lake where he led him into waist-deep water. He quickly grabbed the young man and wrestled him beneath the surface of the water and held him under until he almost drowned. Socrates let the fellow up and waited until he recovered his breathing.

*"What was the first thing you wanted as I held you under water?" Socrates asked.*

*"To breathe!" came the reply.*

*"When you desire wisdom to the same degree that you desire to breathe," said Socrates, "then you may come to me."*

## THE CEREMONY OF EFFORT

Perhaps a sustained drive to acquire inspired wisdom and the enlightened living it is heir to will require dedication on the scale Socrates spoke of. We face so many distractions living and lawyering in our modern world that without the right effort we could fall into a pattern of habitual behavior, doing only what lawyers have been doing for generations. We forget to breathe. In Huston Smith's *World's Religions, A Guide to Our Wisdom Traditions,* he explains that routine ceremony is an effective way to drag ourselves away from uninspired, laborious routine to something better. Smith tells us that the "hallowing of life" through ceremony and ritual adds more dimensions to a life that may have become tedious or humdrum. It helps us to get our breath every now and then.

The Muslim who may find herself looking down as she labors all day is forced to look up and see the towering ceilings of the mosques where she worships. The tedium of her life is thereby interrupted long enough to allow her to *think* about something besides survival and getting ahead. She is coaxed to abandon her need-to-know or survival thinking long enough to form mental images of what a more enlightened life might look like.

Gothic architects set out to create more than mere "height for height's sake" when they built the spires of Notre Dame. They understood that spires help to raise a person's focus from the horizon and *below* to the horizon and *above.* They help separate the nose from the grindstone.

Huston Smith writes that ceremony promotes and sustains not only religion itself, but timeless wisdom as well. Smith emphasizes that some degree of ritualized effort precedes inspiration:

> *The Sabbath eve with its candles and cup of sanctification. The Passover Feast, with its many symbols, the austere solemnity of the Day of Atonement, the ram's horn sounding the new year, the scroll of the Torah adorned with the breastplate and crown—the Jew finds nothing less than the meaning of life in these things, a meaning that spans the centuries in affirming God's great goodness to his people.*

## DOING IT HIS WAY

The type of ceremony Smith is lauding in the foregoing quote would probably be judged by Clarence Darrow as baneful mysticism. His highly developed sense of iconoclasm left him no other choice but to minimize the importance of the inspired wisdom and enlightenment that we are likely to find in our temples, mosques, and churches.

It is apparent that Darrow extracted from his voluminous readings an ardent respect for the *ideas* that are the underpinnings of all the great religious traditions. It is also apparent that he absorbed and applied their timeless lessons in his own life. All the while, however, he shook his fist in the face of those great traditions, for he could not countenance the institutional aspect of religion. He never overcame his blind spot for religious faith. Darrow insisted on looking for his enlightenment in other places, outside the walls and teachings of any church.

The affection that most people feel for the "religion of their nurture" was felt by Clarence Darrow for traveling, and for the sense of inspiration that he experienced in those places. When he was an old man, he wrote:

> *I would like to go to Europe just once more. I would like to cross Trafalgar Square with its hundreds of pigeons being fed by the tourists . . . I would like to saunter over the Thames to the Parliament Building and to awaken in the Metropole Hotel, where I have*

*stayed so many times during the past thirty-odd years, and hear Big Ben boom out the early hours, calling London to be mindful of the flight of time.*

*I would like again to visit Montreux and view the magnificent Alps across the lovely Lac Leman, from the immense windows and the large balcony of the Hotel Beau Rivage, looking out upon the tremendous snow-banked Dents du Midi exactly opposite, like a keystone at the arch of the lake with its steep, sloping, colorful sides; and far away, beyond and above the rest looms Mont Blanc, placid, majestic and unconscious of fleeting time as it has always been.*

*I would like to sit sunning myself in that rare atmosphere, lazily wondering how long the Alps have been there, and how long that beautiful blue lake has reflected the white-capped peaks upon its glassy bosom, and how long, perchance, the scene will continue when I can see it no more.*

As a Journeyman, Darrow broadened and deep-ened his appreciation and understanding of the world by seeing, hearing, and feeling as much of the world as he possibly could. He routinely left his law office, abandoned his tightly wrapped lawyering routine, and traveled the world over to borrow wisdom and inspiration from people, places, and things.

He borrowed from what he heard, what he viewed, and what he touched at Mont Blanc, Montreux, or the Dents du Midi and then shared that inspiration and wisdom with friends, cli-ents, judges, and opponents. What he learned and experienced in those places resurfaced in his *voir dire,* his cross-examinations, his closing statements, and his arguments to judges.

What Darrow failed to see, hear, and feel, un-fortunately, was a kinship with the huge part of the community he served that *did* understand and appreciate the inspired wisdom found in temples, mosques, and churches. Most of the people we serve and advocate for *are* essentially spiritual beings. The type of spirituality that

Darrow dismissed as superfluous mysticism *is* important to our community.

You probably will not be visited this week by an overwhelming number of clients who have recently been spiritually moved by the majestic beauty of the Alps. It is likely, however, that you will have a client in your office who has been moved by what she saw, heard, or felt last weekend in her temple, mosque, synagogue, or church. That client will have found what she believes to be wisdom in those places. We can better serve our clients and ourselves as Journeymen if we avoid developing the type of blind spot Darrow had for ideas that come adorned in ceremonial garb.

**"**

*If I have been charitable*

*in my judgments of my fellow man;*

*if I have tried to help him as best I could . . .*

*I know why I have taken this course*

*—I could not help it.*

*I could have no comfort or peace of mind*

*if I had acted any other way.*

*—Clarence Darrow*

# PART FIVE

## THE SERVANT

Clarence Darrow said of Voltaire, "There is no parallel in history for this great genius." And while Darrow prized highly Voltaire's massive intellect, at the same time he deeply admired and honored Voltaire's commitment to serve others, often at risk of great peril to Voltaire himself. Darrow found him dedicated to the cause of human liberty in that he "never ceased to fight for the cause as long as life remained."

Serving others in a meaningful way seems difficult to accomplish on the busy oval track that most of us lawyers run around in survival mode. Honest service is made all the more difficult because of the field of competitors we find ourselves running with: thoroughbreds bent on winning at any cost—independent, suspicious, and ego-driven to prove themselves right, "in the interest of their clients," of course.

Darrow knew, too, that, although Voltaire was a servant of the people, he was not a "selfless" servant. Darrow told us that Voltaire, in order to do his good work in France two hundred years ago, required the patronage of princes, priests, kings, generals, and influential courtesans. And, while he saw through the shams of courtly life—its "vanities, conceits, cruelties and injustices toward the poor"—Voltaire was not unaffected by the company he kept. Darrow allowed that the man loved fame and was "singularly vain."

Still, Voltaire never stopped assailing the church and state when he deemed them enemies of truth and liberty. He found himself often dodging officers and jailers, and not always successfully.

John P. Altgeld was, like Voltaire, a mentor for Darrow. Altgeld was a populist Chicago politician and lawyer. Darrow spoke passionately about him:

> *The newspapers, the profiteers, the money-mongers, and the pharisees fought him bitterly; but in the humble dwelling-places of the poor, in the factories and mills, among the failures, the misfits and despised, he was worshipped almost as a god. For the maimed and the beaten, the sightless and the voiceless, he was the eyes and ears, and a flaming tongue crying in the wilderness for kindness and humanity and understanding.*

Darrow was deeply moved by the compassion evident in his mentors. His respect for their intelligence was equalled only by his respect for selfless service to others in need.

## PROPPING UP A "GOOD" NAME

It is not surprising in the circles kept by good lawyers that we often find an overdose of selfishness driving even the notion of helping others. It is easy to become, as the Sufis say "man-charmers," when performing in the company of so many snake-charmers. Public gurus, say the Sufis, are man-charmers whose work is to amuse the people in the square, and in the course of it find fame for themselves. You have to look closely, however, to find a *genuine* servant. "The secret saints work for the people," according to Sufi wisdom. Darrow believed his friend John Altgeld was such a man who worked for the people. Voltaire worked for the people, too, but was a bit more the man-charmer than Altgeld.

The secret servant contemplated in Sufi teachings is rare in our profession. It is just as rare in other professions, too, where name recognition and reputation are among the chief means of attracting new clients. Many lawyers would claim "justifiable notoriety" and point to the high costs of living and doing business as a rationale for keeping a high profile when they serve.

## FOR THE SAKE OF SERVICE ITSELF

It is interesting to note that in the tradition of wisdom taught to Zen monks, service to others is considered among the highest *honors.* In fact, in the eight-hundred-year-old *Regulations for Zen Monasteries,* among the six officers listed for each monastery, one is the *tenzo,* a position available only to accomplished, senior monks. This revered person's duty is actually the preparation of meals for the other monks.

The honor bestowed upon the most venerated of all the monks—the great recognition laid at his feet—is not special gifts and high praise. Instead he is given the right, the opportunity, and the duty to *prepare and serve meals* to all the other monks in the monastery. Not just once, but in most cases daily for the rest of his life.

In the *Regulations,* along with pages and pages of instructions on everything from how to wash the vegetables to the manner in which grain weevils are to be removed from the rice, there is this: "Use your way-seeking mind to carefully vary the menus from time to time, *and offer the assembly great ease and comfort.*"Dogen, an eleventh-century Japanese philosopher, wrote this in his journal on the virtue of service and humility:

> *[A priest] was drying some mushrooms in the sun. He had a bamboo stick in his hand and no hat on his head. The sun was very hot, scorching the earth. It looked very painful; his backbone was bent like a bow and his eyebrows were as white as a crane. I went up to the tenzo and asked, "How long have you been a monk?"*
>
> *"Sixty-eight years," he replied.*
>
> *"Why don't you let a helper do this work?"*

The *tenzo* explained that there were no others in the monastery who *should* do the work in his place. The opportunity to serve was his blessing and his honor, not a chore to delegate to others. He points out that he has *earned* the right to serve.

## ON THE OTHER HAND

We may consider how important the concept of service is—even when driven by expectations of personal gain. The Scottish New Testament scholar William Barclay made the comment that "a thing wrongly said can be rightly heard." Scores of wrongs have been made right by lawyers who have served superbly, but with selfish motives. The oppressed have been delivered, the orphans have seen justice, and the pleas of widows heard, no less for having been helped by lawyers with self-serving reasons. Darrow pointed out that selfish motives do, in fact, often serve the common good. In his autobiography, Darrow criticizes the American socialist Henry George for failing to recognize the value of selfish endeavors:

> *The error I found in the philosophy of Henry George was its cocksureness, its simplicity, and the small value it placed upon the selfish motives of men.*

Some would say it was something other than compassion and a sense of justice that drove

Clarence Darrow to fight for eight years through a plethora of appeals and overturned verdicts to finally win an action of replevin for a horse harness worth fifteen dollars. Although Darrow called the case the most important of his early years as a lawyer in Ohio, it probably figures among the most important of his career because of the precedent it established: his bulldog tenacity to win cases, as much for what it meant to himself as to his clients.

Darrow's client—a boy who had been given a harness for attending to the needs of a wealthy man during an illness—paid him five dollars. He tried the case once and lost; tried it again and lost; appealed it to the Court of Common Pleas and won before a jury. The wealthy man had his lawyer take the matter before the Court of Appeals, which reversed the case on a question of law. Even though Darrow had by now moved to Chicago, he appealed to the Supreme Court.

"I wrote the brief, argued the case, paid all expenses, and the court decided in my favor," he said. It is perhaps notable here that Darrow said, in "my" favor, and did not say, "in favor of my client." He declared that there had been no money involved and "not much principle, as I see it now, but then it seemed as if my life depended upon the result." It is a pretty short leap to say that selfish motives drove this case. A right result was nonetheless achieved and exceptional service rendered to the client.

## SERVICE WITH A WHISPER, NOT A SHOUT

But when *does* the heart of a lawyer begin to beat in a rhythm of true service and not in cadence with the ringing of a cash register or the applause of the crowd? In secret. When the real motivation to action is service, the left hand will not know what the right hand has done. The Koran, the New Testament, the Torah, the Doctrine of the Mean, and the wisdom writings within our great religions speak in chorus for the ageless truth of serving in secret.

Even folklore and mythology explore the theme of serving anonymously and lead a thinking person to ponder its value. King Arthur had a special seat at the Round Table for the knight from among his court who found the Holy Grail. The seat was called the "Siege Perilous" and it was under penalty of death that a knight sat undeservingly in the Siege Perilous. Only the greatest of all knights might take this seat of highest honor. It is appropriate that it was Sir Percival, rising from the ranks of innocence and naivety, to finally sit in the Siege Perilous.

The Grail Myth relates a story about Sir Percival's motivation to serve. There is a scene in the great hall of King Arthur's court when, after a successful attempt to find the Holy Grail, Sir Percival is being honored with a great feast. During the height of the ceremonies, the gathering is disrupted by an an old hag who rides straight into the room on a donkey. She wags her finger at Percival, screeching that he is not so great just because sits in the Siege Perilous. "Why, your very own mother died and you did not even attend her funeral!"

The symbolic suggestion is that in the quest for fame and glory, Percival let the true meaning of service die in himself and did not even notice its passing. Percival had performed for the love of the prize of honor among his fellow knights. He had not beaten his foes in a love of service.

Some cynical philosophers have even suggested that the tiniest deed done in the service of others has at its base selfish reasons. We want to feel good about ourselves and so we lend a helping hand for that reason primarily. How many of us would stop to assist in the changing of a stranger's flat tire on a rainy stretch of interstate highway and not go straight home and tell our wife or family members of the good deed we had done?

## THE REWARD OF SERVICE

No critic of Darrow's could suggest convincingly that Darrow served the public for selfish motives. Historians and biographers have been kind to Clarence Darrow because they recognize the importance of the role he played as a sometimes self-centered but unselfish lawyer. In his autobiography Darrow recalls an event that took place in his life that sounds more like a scene from the Jimmy Stewart movie *It's a Wonderful Life.* It is odd for the passage to appear in any writing by Darrow because of its incongruence with the fatalist-nihilist side of Darrow. In it he recalls perhaps the lowest point in his life. He had spent his every dime defending himself against a charge of jury tampering, and, although he was acquitted, he was despondent, tired, and broke from the battle.

> *I felt discouraged and disheartened. That night I received a telegram which read as follows: "St. Louis, Missouri. Clarence Darrow, Los Angeles, California: I hear that you have spent most of your life defending men for nothing and that you are now broke and facing another trial. I will let you have all the money you need for the case. Am now sending draft for one-thousand dollars. Frederick D. Gardener." My eyes filled with tears.*

Curmudgeon, fatalist, iconoclast—all these terms have been used to describe Darrow. He may have been all those things. But on that day he wept to discover such kindness directed toward him, a tribute. That day his tears washed away the façade of his disbelief in unsolicited compassion and reward for selfless service. Darrow may have gone on record doubting as mystical nonsense the teachings of the likes of Buddha, Mohammed, or Paul when they spoke of getting back what we give, but in this instance he lived the proof of the ancient wisdom. And it moved him to tears.

Robert Blanchard, in 1994, won an award from his bar association honoring his commitment to *pro bono* work in his community. Robert offers these reflections:

> *I first began focusing on pro bono work with the mindset that it would be a personal experiment. It was, for me, new and unexplored territory. I was curious about what the basics of service really were. To what degree must I accept and learn genuine humility? I was not at all sure what the costs or consequences of true, unselfish service would be. And, for that matter, whether or*

not I would be able to meet the test. My vision of service was, at best, myopic 14 years ago in law school. The concept of true service was no more than casually mentioned in ethics class. It was one of those "greater good" notions that seemed far less important at the time than finding a job and making my way as a young lawyer. The first few years of law practice did nothing to correct my distorted view of service.

*But my first experience with services rendered without receiving a fee helped to wake me up and allowed me to see things differently. The best analogy I can give is one of the fearful traveler who is being led by a guide over a bridge that connects two mountains. The fearful traveler is uneasy and shaken as he crosses the bridge, his eyes are locked in focus on the abyss below. The guide cries out to the traveler, "Look up, see the mountains." I had begun, finally, to look up from my worries about working for free and saw that something worthwhile was happening for my clients and for me.*

Think back to the last time you did something for someone else without expecting something in return. If it's a struggle to recall an example, don't become self-critical, just decide to "do better" by doing even some small thing for someone. Something as seemingly inconsequential as listening closely and with your full attention to what a child is trying to tell you meets the criteria for an unselfish act.

We have all worked with law partners and associates who, God bless them, will never see any relationship between random acts of unrecognized service and kindness toward others and an improvement in the quality of their own lives. Their linear thinking leads them to believe that people are "only as important as what they can do for me today." We all know lawyers who we believe began thinking this way around age five, and who look as though they will keep it up until they hit age sixty-five.

## COME SEE WHAT I HAVE DONE

A New Orleans poet by the name of Walter Darring, in *My Life's Work*, takes a satirical look in "The Establishment" at our need to be recognized—the poet for his aesthetic genius, and we lawyers, perhaps, for every act of service and every act of kindness that we do.

> *I hereby establish a school of poetry;*
> *It shall be hereinafter known to all*
> *As the Walter Darring School of Poetry.*
>
> *There shall be raised on the grounds of said*
>    *school*
> *A monument to my own magnificence;*
> *It shall be named the Monument*
> *Of the Walter Darring School of Poetry.*
>
> *And there shall be sculpted and set thereon*
> *A statue of the Founder of the school;*
> *It shall be known as the*
> *Winged Orpheus Descending the Monument*
> *Of the Walter Darring School of Poetry.*
>
> *And there shall be set aside a holiday*
> *Upon which diverse students, men and women,*
> *Shall congregate to sing the Founder's fame;*
> *It shall be called the Baccalaureate Orgy and*

*Libation*
*For the Winged Orpheus Descending the*
*Monument*
*Of the Walter Darring School of Poetry.*


*And every year in perpetuity*
*The Founder shall, in whatsoever form please*
*him*
*Appear and bless the company;*
*It shall be honored as the Miracle*
*Of the Disembodied Mind at the Baccalaureate*
*Orgy*
*And Libation for the Winged Orpheus*
*Descending The Monument*
*Of the Walter Darring School of Poetry.*

As intoxicating as it can be to massage our sense of self-worth, even to the extremes our poet intends, in truth we must accomplish what Clarence Darrow suggested in the epigraph for Part Three: "All triumphs are futile without the victory over self." He suggests, too, that it is simply a life lived under honest self-scrutiny that will yield the victory we seek, not the approval and company of saints and indebted dignitaries.

## LOOKING TO CHANGE THINGS

If we are willing to look beneath the image we have of ourselves as lawyers and beneath the image others may have of us, to get beyond mere image preservation, we may be surprised to find, as Darrow suggested, "within our breast a heart of flint."

If we keep observing ourselves with a fearless eye, watching the manner in which we interact within our profession, if we simply admit to having emotions like ego and pride and we can honestly see them at work in ourselves, then we are taking the first important step in cultivating a heart for service.

Darrow declared that the fearless and honest appraisal of what lies beneath a lawyer's well-kept image is the key to progressing toward a willingness to serve others. The very scrutiny takes this "hard and pulseless thing and scars and twists and melts it in a thousand tortuous ways until the stony mass is purged and softened and is sensitive to every touch." As improbable as it may seem, the simple act of *honestly* looking at ourselves is a more powerful agent of change than trying to warp ourselves into becoming who we are not.

Genuine humility and unselfish service may not, at first glance, be attractive to those of us who lawyer for a living. The good news is that our services, even if lacking humility and altruism, can benefit society all the same. The bad news is that it is only *we* who fail to derive the maximum benefit from serving others when it is not done selflessly.

Unless we become at least curious about such concepts, unless we "look up to see the mountain"we may never become aware of the breathtaking mountain view. It is the actual ascension to those crests, not the longing look toward them, that affords the traveler his highest and broadest vision.

## WALKING THE TALK

In the *History of God,* Karen Armstrong said that new ideologies that developed during the Axial Age—giving rise to the wisdom traditions—all insisted that the test of authenticity for religious experience was that it be integrated successfully into daily life. "After enlightenment, a man or woman must return to the marketplace and practice compassion for all living things." In a word, *service.*

But Armstrong made a rather strong indictment when she editorialized that "the religion of compassion is followed only by a minority; most religious people are content with decorous worship in synagogue, church, temple and mosque." Whether or not that is true, it *is* true that observing decorum is not wisdom. You may be assured, too, that you cannot just sit around and have inspired wisdom drop in your lap.

## CAN WE GET THERE FROM HERE?

Since not many of us are likely to leave our law offices and business suits behind in favor of the monastery and a woolen robe, we have to wonder how the concept of serving others would play out in the life we are living now. For a lawyer in our chaotic Western culture, which values "I" over "Thou" by a broad margin, just what would be the tangible results of a shift or transformation away from "me" to a commitment of service? What would it mean in everyday practice to observe a *tenzo*-like calling where selfless service to others carries its own intrinsic reward and honor?

That is obviously not my call to make where you are concerned. It is not my purpose to prescribe behavior for the readers. What this book does is to offer ideas and opinions from diverse sources about the merits of a journey toward more enlightened living for lawyers. If application of these ideas seems in some way worthwhile to you, if they appeal to you as a means for achieving better ends in your lawyering life, it is entirely your choice as to how you will employ them. This is only a road map that points out a few different ways to get home.

Matthew, the Christian apostle and Gospel author, left his readers with a most befuddling, confounding image of what they should do to live richer, fuller lives as leaders in their community. He told them that according to Jesus they must become servants in order to become leaders. He told them the same thing that the Buddhist *tenzo* lives by: A wise, accomplished, and enlightened leader is one who is also a servant. Darrow might have objected to the teachings of prophets, apostles, and monks at one time or another in his life, but he nevertheless wrote these words late in his life:

> *I have done this [lawyering] for those who paid me, and for those who gave me nothing, and often have spent my own money to provide for the defense. I have never let the lack of money stand in the way of helping people in trouble. I am sure that I have given at least half of my time and services to this kind of work without any financial reward. . . . My only regret is that I have not been able to do more.*

**"**

*I doubt if I would recommend anything
if I thought my advice
was to be followed.*

—*Clarence Darrow*

**"**

## PART SIX

---

## THE TEACHER

As we advance in wisdom's curriculum, we should find ourselves overriding our ego with maturity. We should also assume the Journeyman's commitment to discovery, cultivate a heart for anonymous service, and recognize that our hearts as lawyers should beat with the same moral and ethical rhythm both inside and outside our offices. After all that, we should arrive at a level of development that motivates us to share all that we have learned. We must become Teachers.

This chapter is not devoted to discussing how to teach *voir dire* techniques, or methods for delivering opening and closing statements. It is about the Journeyman sharing what she learns about the journey, about ego, service, and developing a right livelihood. It is about sharing wisdom about lawyering and living; sharing wisdom that you have struggled to understand; sharing it with those still engaged in the struggle.

The role of the teacher, as a step on the path to the level of wisdom this book sets out to describe, is not taken to mean standing at a lectern—although these opportunities will certainly arise for the teacher. Nor does the teaching role we imagine belong only to the "elders." Darrow wrote:

> *Experience can only come from one's own life. No one can live any other life, or really understand any other. He cannot even understand his own. No doubt Methuselah mourned over the shortcomings of the young who had lived but a few of his nine-hundred and sixty odd years. But years do not necessarily develop wisdom.*

Darrow was correct, inasmuch as a mere chronological advance to the point of one's death in no way promises the achievement of wisdom and enlightened living. The world's great religions concur, teaching that strong desire and untiring effort *coupled* with experience allow us to recognize, understand, and apply new insights to our lives. Age is not a criterion for, nor a promise of, wisdom.

## WHO MAY TEACH? WHO MAY BE TAUGHT?

Darrow's idea that no one may learn from the advice and life experiences of others belies the entire framework of human evolution. Passing on wisdom from generation to generation preserves and magnifies what mankind has figured out along the way. Jesus and Mohammed, Aristotle and Plato, Greek and Roman mythology, the arts and literature, all have cried out for saner choices and wiser courses of human action. Many within our ranks have listened to the advice. They are aware of saner choices. They know about wiser and more enlightened ways to live as lawyers. They act upon what they know. Now they must teach what they have learned. Everyone treading wisdom's path must join his or her voice, and more importantly, the *example* of his or her life to the chorus that both enlightens and warns fellow travelers where they themselves may safely step and where the certain dangers lie. It is a responsibility, not an option.

Paul Benton has been practicing law in Mississippi for 17 years. He shares a few thoughts about lawyers as teachers:

> *When I first began attending seminars for continuing legal education, I was often amused by what I call the "program peacocks." They typically walked around the entire week with multi-colored ribbons decorating their suits or dresses. These ribbons were their badges of accomplishments. They advertised to those attending the seminar that they were the honored speakers, officers, the movers and shakers. Their efforts at impressing me about who they were sometimes interfered with their ability to teach me how to become a better young lawyer.*

*Invariably, however, I came away from those programs inspired, enlightened, and informed because of the unselfish attention I received from some experienced, seasoned veteran of a lawyer who invited me to have dinner or drinks while we both shared our experiences as lawyers. These veteran lawyers and teachers all share some common traits. They listen before they speak. They speak without posturing, and they are jubilant if they see that their advice has helped another lawyer.*

## THE TEACHER *ALSO* LEARNS

Paul Benton's experience illustrates some important concepts about teaching. In recognizing the need for sharing what we have learned about living and lawyering, we must be willing to *bend down* to teach rather than tower over the pupil. We must *listen* two to three times longer than the time we devote to speaking. We must believe that we *learn* by teaching. We must be *patient.*

## WALK THE TALK

And, finally, the most difficult and most important concept we must remember is that we must live what we teach. The Chinese refer to Confucius as the First Teacher. He had developed a method of teaching that he labeled "constancy." Simply put, it meant that the Teacher must match his deeds to his words. In one of the many dialogues between Confucius and his students, Confucius was asked how a wise man might be recognized:

> *He acts before he speaks, and afterwards, speaks according to his actions . . . At first, my way with men was to hear their words, and give them credit for their conduct. Now my way is to hear their words, and look at their conduct . . . A man without constancy cannot be either a wizard or a doctor . . . Inconstant in his virtue, he will be visited with disgrace.*

## ON THE YELLOW BRICK ROAD

The legal profession has in place a well-honed methodology for teaching new associates and young partners the basics for "surviving" and progressing financially as a lawyer. This "teaching" we make reference to is a noun, not a verb. Not much if any teaching is actually involved. We generally fail to apply many of the principles of teaching listed above. Young lawyers simply observe some outdated rules that have been handed down for generations: bill more hours, post more fees, and receive a bigger bonus; show up very early and leave very late—and thereby be noticed; be accepted by preserving and perpetuating the image of lawyering handed down to you.

A better lesson to learn as a young lawyer would be to understand the "Oz Syndrome." Failure to grasp and accept the fact that the Oz Syndrome exists can stifle the teacher-student relationship and seriously impair the teacher's ability to teach and the student's ability to learn.

The Oz Syndrome works like this: On one hand, you have a not-very-well adjusted little man behind a curtain manipulating controls that make him appear bigger than life, very wise, worldly, and important—very "senior partnerish." On the other hand, you have the citizens of Oz nurturing and promoting the little man's illusion with their unquestioning acceptance of the image they are presented.

## PEEK BEHIND THE CURTAIN

Young lawyers would be well-advised to do what Dorothy did in Oz—lift the curtain and take a critical look at the person with the controls in his hands, and recognize that in reality there are no wizards. Teaching and learning begin with honest and open interaction between the teacher and the student. Artificial walls that are created out of the combination of ego and insincere hero worship interfere with that process. A law office is an inappropriate setting for smoke and mirrors if the senior partners really want to teach, and the associates really want to learn.

An authentic Teacher is not given to self-gratifying posturing. This Teacher realistically has the ability to nullify the ego-drenched caste system that, in the setting of most law firms, has been handed down for generations. Such a system is simply outdated.

C. S. Lewis wrote a play called *Loki Bound.* In the play, Thor with his hammer and his threats was constantly complaining that Loki did not pay proper respect to the gods; Thor complained that Loki did not recognize their heroic powers; to which Loki replied, "I pay respect to wisdom, not to strength."

## Most Heroes Live in Hollywood

Darrow left lessons for both the teacher and the student who are not caught up in the Oz Syndrome. Clarence Darrow had precious few people in his life who rose to the level of hero. Primarily because he never went looking for heroes. He lived by principles that required him to question authority. He was constantly raising the curtain on would-be wizards, and became in the course of it a man of true principles, self-sufficient and self-reliant. Most of his values were "hand-wrought." Darrow followed the Confucian principle of constancy. When he picked his teachers, their words and deeds had to match. He was not a "yes man." He did not see wizards where no wizards existed. Some older individual who was further up the pecking order was just that, but not more, unless it was truly deserved. For Darrow, grey hair, longevity, and position only counted when accompanied by real wisdom.

## FINDING NUGGETS WITHIN THE SILT

Mike Eidson is a superb trial lawyer from Miami, Florida. He understands the principle of constancy, and he is a respected teacher within our profession. Eidson, throughout his legal career, has picked his teachers the way Darrow did. He writes about one of his teachers:

> *This year, I gave the eulogy for one of the most important teachers in my life. From the minute I met Bill Hicks as a young associate, I recognized that I wasn't having to force myself to see a mentor, a leader, even a hero, where one did not exist. He was the real thing.*
>
> *I listened to Bill and honored his advice, not because it was professionally expedient to do*

so, but because his quality of character was easy to respect.

He was a great teacher because he led the way for almost everyone around him to discover the best in themselves. Lawyers wanted to be around Bill not because of his great professional success, not because of what he could do for them as a lawyer, but because of the terrific blueprint his life offered them. A blueprint for selflessness, balance, spirituality, and wisdom. No young lawyer needed to insincerely overmagnify the importance of Bill Hicks as a teacher.

His ego did not require such insincerity, as is often the case with older, successful lawyers. He would offer what he knew to any young lawyer who genuinely wanted to learn. What he offered to teach them was not so much how to be a great lawyer, but more how to be a decent, balanced, and wise human being. He taught young lawyers the lesson that most world-class lawyers have taught. He taught that being an exceptional *lawyer is only part of the total package. He taught that we must look for more in our lives.*

In Clarence Darrow's entire life, there is only one person besides his father who could be viewed as a true mentor to Darrow. That person was John Altgeld. Darrow was wise enough to recognize that we may learn a little from everyone if we are paying attention, but he was extremely selective about whom he chose to mentor him. Mentoring is one notch up the scale from teaching because of the long and close association it implies.

Darrow devoted the last few pages of his autobiography to reprinting his eulogy for Altgeld. Darrow did not create or imagine an image of Altgeld in an attempt to create a hero where one did not exist. Darrow, in everything he wrote about Altgeld, was quick to point out Altgeld's many shortcomings.

The reason Darrow developed such love and respect for Altgeld began with the fact that

Darrow did not go looking for a teacher without first developing his own core value system. Darrow knew first how he wanted to live his life before asking the question; "Is there someone out there constant enough and wise enough to be a role model for me, who can help me better learn how to live and lawyer?"

Darrow's predefined, carefully constructed self-image allowed him to seek out a mentor who might help him remain faithful to that image. For example, Darrow's heart and sympathies were squarely on the side of the less fortunate, the oppressed, life's underclass. Therefore, he looked to Altgeld to show him how to live as a lawyer who embraced those values.

Darrow knew what he wanted to become before he began borrowing ideas, images, and blueprints from Altgeld. If Altgeld had lived and lawyered in a way that was inconsistent with Darrow's well-developed value system, Darrow might have called him a friend, or necessary business partner, but he would not have been a teacher or mentor to Darrow in any serious way.

The relationship that developed between Darrow and Altgeld was dependent on how well the teacher's values meshed with the student's.

Very often, young associates and partners do the opposite of what Darrow did in choosing his mentor. They approach lawyering without much of a mission statement about what they want to become. Their values in lawyering—and living—end up mirroring the core values of the more powerful and dominant lawyers within their professional circle regardless of what those values might be. It is often a case of image making at its worst, by default almost.

For young lawyers caught up in such a process, all that glitters takes on the appearance of gold. They begin their career without a clear image of what they want to become, aside from becoming wealthy and professionally successful. They seldom engage in the process of seeking out a mentor or a teacher. More often they are looking for a hero or a star to whom they can attach themselves. Someone who has gone before them and "made it" is among their most important criteria.

## SOME GOLD IS GOING UNDISCOVERED

On the other hand, there are potentially thousands of Darrows looking for Altgelds within our lawyering community. A great many lawyers do have a vision about what they want to become beyond mere financial and professional success. They want to grow as spouses, parents, and community leaders. They want to grow spiritually and intellectually. By the time they hang out their shingle, most of them have been overachievers for over twenty-five years. They enter the community of lawyering with a fairly sophisticated sense of what kind of person and lawyer they would like to become as their lives and their careers continue to develop.

In the '90s, a huge number of young lawyers are graduating from law school and courageously choosing to hang their shingle on the wall of their own law practice. They make that choice only in part because the market has forced them to do so. Many do so because they are committed to meshing their non-lawyer life with their lawyering life in a way that preserves their quality of living. These folks are not looking for wizards or heroes to help them make their way. If we are to nurture our profession to its "full bloom of excellence," we must not fail those who sincerely seek help to become the best lawyering has to offer. Which means they need teachers and mentors who offer them real substance, not form. If we have gained some wisdom along the way in our lives as lawyers and we want to teach others what we have learned, it might help us to analyze what Darrow said about his mentor, John Altgeld:

> *We who knew the man, who had clasped his hand and heard his voice, and looked into his smiling face; we who knew his life of kindliness, of charity, of infinite pity to the outcast and the weak; we who knew his human heart, could never be deceived. A truer, greater, gentler, kindlier soul has never lived and died.*

## TEACHING WITH A HUMAN HEART

The kindly, gentle soul that Darrow saw in Altgeld is not easily located among the typical group of senior partners or even mid-level partners in most law firms. Arrogance and a perpetuation of the Oz Syndrome often prevent the experienced senior partner in both average and small law firms from growing into the role of Teacher or mentor. Unfortunately, many truly have very little to offer younger lawyers except some self-aggrandizing war stories here and there.

Self-centered, self-aggrandizing image preservation is difficult to abandon. If it were not so, we would find thousands of John Altgelds within our professional ranks. Instead we find too many lawyers who seem hopelessly trapped by their own sense of self-importance. We have spent a lifetime creating images that make us appear powerful, authoritative, influential, forceful. In fact we often show a severe countenance that masquerades as wisdom. We attempt to conduct our lives from a position of strength. We believe that survival within our testosterone-driven profession does not permit showing our "human heart" to those who are lower down the pecking order within our professional circle.

The following anecdote by a lawyer who will be identified only as J. P. provides a lesson about teaching:

> *Several years ago, my ego and distorted sense of self-importance almost resulted in the resignation of one of the most talented young lawyers I have ever worked with. He was second-chairing a complicated product liability case. He had been in the trenches preparing the case. He had a superb command of the facts, the strategy, and the law.*
>
> *Several times during the pretrial conference on the case, I commandeered his presentation, more in an attempt to assert my own self-importance than to add any meaningful substance to his presentations. It was an almost unconscious attempt to impress upon the opposing counsel and the judge that I was the "big dog" in charge of the case. I was his senior partner. If this important case was to be won, it would be won through my strength and my talent, not his.*

*This talented young lawyer handed me his resignation shortly after the case was resolved. He told me that I had failed to respect that he had a self-image of his own. He pointed out in his written resignation that he wanted to learn, but he did not want to be incessantly cajoled and admonished by the heavy hand of a lawyer whose ego made the process of learning impossible.*

*His letter of resignation pointed out that I was afraid to hand the reins over to him because my sense of self-importance would not allow me to do so. He artfully painted a picture of me through his well-chosen, heartfelt words. It was a picture, not of a teacher, but of an insecure, arrogant, elder lawyer who had become blinded by with his sense of self-importance. I have always heard that the most wonderful gift someone can give you is a picture that describes how you are seen by others. It was painful to look at that picture. I was not a teacher, a mentor, or even a decent friend to this young superstar of a lawyer. In fact, he had become the instructor and I had become the pupil.*

*That letter to this day is a prized possession of mine. It was a first step toward learning how to become a teacher.*

## THE IN AND OUT OF PALACE WALLS

Pride, *amour-propre,* and arrogance all factor into the process of keeping apart the potential teacher and the potential student. The experienced, more financially successful lawyer often intentionally creates her own palace walls as a tribute to herself. After building those walls, she often then pulls up the drawbridge that crosses the moat surrounding her palace. At last, she has "arrived," but at the same time she has isolated herself from the very people she is best equipped to help—those still engaged in the struggle.

Buddha, Jesus, Confucius, and Mohammed all understood the importance of moving "outside the palace walls" in order to become an effective teacher. Palace walls separate us from would-be students who might benefit from our message. According to legend, Indian Prince

Siddhartha Guatama sneaked outside his palace walls one day and was forever changed by what he saw. He saw his fellow countrymen struggling to overcome the burden of living day to day in a harsh world. He had never seen illness, old age, poverty, and the like before that day because his father, in a misguided attempt to shelter him from seeing misery and suffering, had not allowed him outside the palace walls.

What he saw made Siddhartha leave his palace to become a Journeyman, intent on learning anything and everything that would help him teach his countrymen to raise themselves up from their struggle. Siddhartha, of course, became the Buddha and with his enlightenment also learned how to teach. His message is still being received by Buddhists all over the world.

Once you decide to remain outside the palace, once you commit to helping others by teaching them, you will be aided in your effort by following a few time-tested principles of teaching. The lessons of the world's great teachers are not copyrighted intellectual property requiring permission for use. Here are a few teaching principles that you may use freely:

## TEACH AS THOUGH THE QUALITY OF YOUR LIFE DEPENDED ON IT

Clarence Darrow late in life became one of the most sought-after lecturers in America. He said he enjoyed debating and lecturing about social, political, and religious problems because of what it did for *him*. Darrow said:

> *I realize that what really drew me to these endeavors was the self-satisfaction that I got out of it all, and so I am aware that it has not been a desire to help my fellows nearly so much as to gratify certain feelings of my own.*

Darrow recognized what most Teachers recognize, that the teacher comes away with as much for himself as he leaves for the student. The Journeyman who has advanced to the level of Teacher might easily recognize that he is actually presenting lessons in order that he too may better learn the lesson. It becomes easier to maintain humility and avoid a sanctimonious attitude when the teacher understands that he is still learning the lesson he is sharing with others.

## FEET ON GROUND, HEAD OUT OF CLOUDS

The teacher must not tower over the student. Idries Shah is an extremely prolific Sufi writer. In his book *The Commanding Self* he writes:

> *There are certain characteristics which run through teachership... If you are teaching a student something which you know and he does not, you have to draw yourself to what you call his level, and pull him up slowly.*

In order to understand, to see clearly *where* and at *what level* the prospective student stands, you must first truthfully assess where *you* stand. Which way are *you* looking? Up? Or are you looking down at your student?

A teacher must learn to see herself as others see her. You must be able, figuratively speaking, to stand three persons back in a grocery store checkout line and observe whether you are patient or impatient. You must observe yourself and decide whether you are compassionate, arrogant, understanding, pompous, or a blend of all the above. It is important to know whether or not your self-appraisal looks anything like the appraisal given to you by those you wish to teach. The messenger must mirror the message.

## DO NOT FEAR REJECTION

The overwhelming majority of people you may want to teach will not hear your message either because they don't want to hear it, or because at the time you deliver it they are not ready to hear and understand. A Teacher must leave the synthesis and application of what she teaches to the one being taught. And in some cases, it may be years later that the meaning of the lesson becomes clear. Clarence Darrow wrote that the grandchild cannot learn from the grandfather because the child lacks any experiential basis for possible understanding. As the grandchild grows and matures, however, a grandfather's words have a way of echoing. Understanding a grandfather's wisdom may eventually come from that echo.

Once when Buddha was teaching before a crowd, someone asked him to explain the meaning of life. He did not answer with words but simply held a lotus blossom above his head for a moment. Only one listener in the crowd bowed his head in understanding. How many of the listening crowd, however, in the years that followed finally bowed their heads in understanding of that powerful image? Moses, too, acknowledged that most of what he tried to teach would be slow to take hold. He accepted the fact that that was the best he could hope for. He wrote:

> *May my teaching drop as the rain, my speech distill as the dew, the gentle rain upon the tender grass.*

Jesus of Nazareth uses the parable of the sower, the parable of the mustard seed, and the parable of the weeds to illustrate that very little of what we teach is immediately heard, understood, or accepted. The teacher must simply be patient, and confident that time and experience will fill in the gaps and aid the learning process. You have met the requirements of the role of teacher when you have sincerely attempted to show someone an improved way, a more logical way to enlightened living in lawyering.

## KEEP IT SIMPLE, SAGE

Some lessons have remained ageless in part because of the simplicity of the message. James T. Fisher, a teacher and psychiatrist, wrote:

> *If you were to take the sum total of all the authoritative articles ever written by the most qualified of psychologists and psychiatrists on the subject of mental hygiene—if you were to combine them and refine them and cleave out the excess verbiage—if you were to . . . have these unadulterated bits of pure scientific knowledge concisely expressed by the most capable of living poets, you would have an awkward and incomplete summation of the Sermon on the Mount.*

Wisdom's complexity does not lie in details; wisdom is evasive only in *application.* Comprehending an idea like "service" does not require the same intellectual skill required to get a handle on Einstein's "relativity within the space-time continuum." Relativity works automatically in the universe; service to others works only when *put* to work. Wisdom isn't hard to grasp; our complicity with its principles is the hard part.

Zen Buddhists use parables to shed light on a belief that many people are enlightened, but wish that they were not. For example, a man may know that he should be merciful and compassionate. He may already recognize the advantage of humility over arrogance. In his head, it may be clear that he should forgive and love his neighbors. These are not difficult concepts to comprehend. The Zen Buddhist argues that many people choose to ask questions, to appear ignorant, in fact, about what they already know because they want to avoid the behavior required of these simple truths. They take refuge in the question. They already know the answer.

Likewise, there will be very few ethical or moral dilemmas a lawyer will ever face where he does not already know the correct answer long before he poses the question about what to do. The role of the teacher, therefore, becomes simple. The teacher is merely there to point the way down a path that, upon deep reflection, begins to look *familiar* to the student.

Darrow went so far as to criticize those who wished to take credit for "leading" others. He believed that there was a sovereignty of knowledge within each individual:

> *Believing that men and women do what was set down for them to do and was indestructibly woven through the whole warp and woof of life, I come to but one conclusion— no one deserves either praise or blame.*

## FROM SMALL STEPS TO QUANTUM LEAPS

The skilled Teacher never loses sight of the big picture. He is, in fact, motivated by a vision of what the big picture could someday look like. He believes that his vision of the big picture can materialize and be made more promising through a series of sometimes minimal efforts on his part. He believes in synergy. Ken Keyes best explains the type of synergy the Teacher believes in in *The 100th Monkey*. Keyes tells the story of a study conducted on an island in the South Pacific. Specific social habits of groups of wild monkeys inhabiting that island were analyzed over a period of years. In the course of the study, the scientist began feeding the monkeys sweet potatoes.

Keyes tells the story of how one monkey developed a habit of washing his sweet potato before eating it. Later, a dozen more monkeys began doing the same. Later, a dozen more monkeys, and then a dozen more, and a dozen more until all the monkeys on that island were washing their sweet potatoes. In fact, oddly, monkeys on another isolated island fifty miles away were soon observed washing their potatoes. Keyes obviously didn't bother to write *The 100th Monkey* so we could learn about the hygiene of primates. Some have even suggested that the monkeys were dunking their potatoes in the seawater because they liked the salty taste. The book's importance lies in the possibility of extrapolating data and drawing conclusions from the behavior of monkeys that suggest correlations and dynamic possibilities for our own human behavior. Particularly, about the sharing of important ideas and how they can begin in relative isolation and then, with sufficient repetition, make quantum leaps throughout an entire society. The 100th Monkey Principle  suggests that synergy can positively or negatively impact how we live depending on the habit, idea, concept, or message that is being taught on our "island." Here is what Keyes said about monkeys, islands, and sweet potatoes:

> *When a certain number of individuals achieve an awareness of a concept, a spontaneous spreading or ideological breakthrough occurs across all individuals of the group.*

To characterize the breakthrough Keyes speaks of as being a quantum leap in *consciousness* might arouse the cynic to argue that the 100th Monkey Principle is instead a quantum leap of duplication in mere behavioral traits.

That debate aside, the principle observed and recorded by Keyes is not new. It has been restated and redefined hundreds of different ways since the Greeks placed *synergos* (working together) into mankind's vocabulary a millennium ago.

Long before scientists were studying monkeys on isolated islands, the Greeks were giving consideration to what we now refer to as synergy. They said that often the *total* effect of isolated or discrete events is greater or more profound than what we might expect if we were to consider merely the magnitude of each isolated event independently. Jesus suggested, too, that the product of two or more minds joined in a common purpose, attitude, and idea would invite nothing less than divine inspiration.

Teachers may take comfort in knowing that breakthroughs often do occur. Quantum leaps in consciousness for entire groups do take place when the right student connects with the right message. The trick is to "stay on" the simple message.

## JUST PASSING THROUGH

It is said that all good parents hope their children exceed them in every aspect of their lives. Teachers, likewise, strive to have their students occupy a place in the world greater than the place they themselves occupy. The teacher wants his student to do better, travel farther, and receive greater recognition.

It is difficult to teach effectively if after every lesson you look over your shoulder to see if your student is going to catch up, or heaven forbid, pass you. You should *assume* that your student *is* going to be a better lawyer. You should *hope* that her achievements will overshadow your own.

Some older lawyers, however, sometimes try to permanently possess the place they occupy in the world, hanging on with a death grip to the prominence their achievements have given them. They are often completely unwilling to give up their place at the front of the line to make room for new faces or new talent. The older, experienced, successful trial lawyer must acknowledge that he cannot have time stand still to perennially honor his achievements and "place" in the world. When he or she is willing to admit that even magnificent stone monuments to greatness will someday crack and crumble to dust, then real teaching can occur.

*Wisdom cannot come
from listening to the old,
or reading what they say,
but from life alone.*

—*Clarence Darrow*

## Part Seven

---

## The Sage

Throughout the pages of this book, we have sought to map a journey toward the understanding of some simple truths that most lawyers are aware of but don't often take the time to contemplate. We have focused on a few truths that have been presented for centuries in the literature of the world's great religions, truths that the eminent theologian Huston Smith labeled religion's wisdom traditions.

I positively do not presume to have advanced beyond anyone else as a Journeyman lawyer struggling to understand and live these truths. They are much easier to write about than to actually live. However, I am convinced that Clarence Darrow in his eighty-one years *did* advance far beyond most of us in understanding, believing, and living these truths. As I pointed out in the beginning of this book, Darrow tells us he did not need religion of any form or fashion to understand how he should live and lawyer. He got home by another way.

## A ROAD BY ANY OTHER NAME . . .

Darrow, I believe, would agree with the suggestion that lawyers can enjoy a higher and better quality of life, regardless of professional achievements and material wealth, when they accomplish the inner work that allows them to advance spiritually. He would no doubt, however, argue that spirituality is not necessarily a consequence of religious faith. He might point out that he understood the threat of an uncontrolled ego without being a Hindu or a Christian, that he recognized the need to make a living in a socially responsible way without reading the teachings of Mohammed. No doubt in his mind he paid attention to creating for himself a right livelihood without taking inspiration from Buddha's Eightfold Path. He was a good student and a good teacher whether or not he ever studied Confucius.

There is no doubt that many who have spent time studying and analyzing the complexities of Darrow's unusual character would not call him a Sage. I believe Clarence Darrow was a Sage. Identifying a Sage is something akin to identifying a great work of art: Van Gogh's "Starry Night" may be the work of a great visionary to one art lover and leave another unmoved. Or it may be similar to finding a "correct" philosophy: On one hand, Socrates' logical analysis sounded like great philosophy to his faithful students; and on the other hand, his critics only heard the words of a heretic who was leading his youthful followers astray. Likewise, common ground is difficult to find for agreement upon whom we may label "Sage."

There are a whole host of reasons why many would argue that Darrow fell *far* short of what they would call a Sage. His interpersonal and familial relationships were sometimes poor, at best. His cynicism and fatalism made him appear at times—to some observers—shallow, obstinant, and harsh. His love of debate and argument, his readiness to join in the "battle"—wherever he found it—all would seem to belie any real measure of inner peace.

If those criteria take him off your list of Sage candidates, Clarence Darrow possessed other characteristics in common with ones we would probably agree to call Sage. In this section we will discuss those personal qualities, following which Clarence Darrow may look like a thorny bush with flowers, or he may look like a rose. My judgment about Darrow reflects my own attitudes and beliefs about him.

## THE FREEDOM TO CHOOSE

One characteristic of Sages is that they seem to place a higher value or priority on their personal freedom, far more than most of us. They are willing to make extraordinary compromises to develop and maintain that freedom. They are willing to walk down the "road less traveled" to get to that freedom.

Sogyal Rinpoche is a Tibetan Buddhist who wrote *The Tibetan Book of Living and Dying.* In his book, Rinpoche includes a twenty-five line poem by Portia Nelson. In it the poet cleverly expresses the potential for escaping self-imposed, habitual patterns for living. Only after such escape is there a chance for free flight to true freedom of choice. Nelson describes a person who keeps falling in the same hole in the same sidewalk, over and over again, until the realization dawns that there is another choice available, and has been available all along. The last line of the poem reads: "I walk down a different street."

Nelson's poem carries a beautiful message, a message of liberation and hope also expressed by Jesus, known by the Hindu, extolled by the Buddhist and the Sufi: Our personal freedom begins when we make choices that are unburdened by habitual, rote-and-note responses from the past. When we can do this, we have also learned to reject hand-me-down images that are planned, packaged, and sold to us by the rest of the world. If you continue to act the way you have been led to believe a lawyer *should* act, you are committed to falling in the same old hole time after time.

Darrow isolated himself from hand-me-down lawyer images by proclaiming himself to be a nihilist and iconoclast. In setting himself apart from the crowd he preserved his "freedom-friendly" self-image and rejected most of what the rest of the world honored and coveted. He was a twentieth-century Diogenes, discarding provincial-mindedness. Clarence Darrow was not only adept at avoiding potholes, he was free to choose a different street—and *did*—when that other street better suited his journey.

In Irving Stone's six hundred–page *Darrow for the Defense*, he describes Clarence Darrow:

> *[Darrow was] a sentimental cynic. He was a gullible skeptic. He was an organized anarchist. He was a happy pessimist. He was a modest egocentric. He was a hopeful defeatist. And*

*was aware of the various contradictions he was housing under one dome.*

Throughout his book, Stone describes Darrow as a man who is obsessed with the need to be free from the confining habits and traditions that are in such great demand by the rest of the world. Stone quotes a statement of Darrow's that illustrates his steadfast self-reliance:

*I can say with perfect honesty that I have never knowingly catered to anyone's ideas, and I have expressed what was within me, regardless of consequences.*

According to Stone, Darrow "liked people alive on the face of the earth, caring little about their titles, position, wealth or other external appurtenances." Not so with most of the rest of us. An experienced "great lawyer" told me:

*I would be dishonest if I did not admit that the way I live both in my personal life and in my professional life is a detailed reflection of the way my older peers conduct their lives. I don't enjoy golf, but I am a member of a country club. I live in a home with more rooms than my family will ever occupy. I could not possibly wear all of the expensive suits I own. I have almost neurotically tried to surround myself with powerful and influential people rather than with friends. I've owned boats, planes, automobiles, vacation homes, and exclusive club memberships because to be able to possess such things has helped me convey that I certainly must be a "great lawyer" and a "great human being."*

## THINGS: WHO OWNS WHOM?

To suggest that affluence and wisdom are mutually exclusive positions is far-fetched and unreasonable. It is not unreasonable, however, to suggest that the Sage is not a prisoner to whatever affluence she enjoys. She might drive an expensive BMW, but her sense of self-worth does not "ride" on the BMW. Her self-image is not shaped by an automobile. A Sage might indeed purchase a condo. But the keys to the condo in no way hold the key to her self-image. I read a story years ago about a banker who felt that he was about to knuckle under to the stresses and high-pressure lifestyle of his job. So he quit. He studied theology and did volunteer work for several years. But then, finally, he returned to his old job in the banking industry. He again wore three-piece suits. He was once again living the affluent lifestyle that he had left behind years earlier. There was, however, one key difference. The banker explained that he had learned during his sabbatical "to *do* what one chooses without *being* what is done." He had put aside the well-honed, highly developed mold that bankers "should" adopt. He had acquired the freedom to go into a bank on a daily basis, to discuss money, to trade money, to lend money, to dress the part, and to do his job even better than before . . . and yet not *be* a banker.

## A SOLOMON BY ANY OTHER NAME . . .

King Solomon, over the centuries, has maintained a status of being the poster boy for wisdom. In addition to being one of the wealthiest kings living on the earth in 950 B.C., Solomon certainly could be considered one of the great intellects living during that period. Religious and secular critics alike would have to agree that Solomon at least *looked* like a Sage.

Solomon is credited with being the author of the Old Testament book of Ecclesiastes. Solomon, the philosopher, devotes a huge amount of ink in Ecclesiastes to explaining why our efforts to possess, own, and acquire wealth, fame, and power fritter away an inordinate amount of our life energy. Solomon thought that what we should really pay attention to is how to "eat, drink, and be happy."

The message of Ecclesiastes reads like fatalism, and cynicism at its worst. Solomon used harsh, bleak vocabulary, imagery, and metaphor in an attempt to distill a few drops of wisdom that he had acquired in his long, colorful life. While analyzing common characteristics of the Sage, it cannot hurt to compare notes with Solomon. Solomon's advice that we should eat, drink and enjoy life probably is not a recommendation to approach living and lawyering with wild, reckless abandon. A hangover in 950 B.C. was as miserable as a hangover in 1997. It might seem easier to analyze Solomon's message after reading the following thoughts from Larry Morris about our inability as lawyers to enjoy the moment, our failure to remember that we are, after all, only "passing through," moment by moment.

*Last year, I took my family snow skiing in Colorado. Our mountain cabin overlooked a breathtakingly beautiful range of snow-covered mountains. Almost every moment of the short vacation was visually idyllic. However, most of the trip, I occupied my mind with how I could go about owning part of this beautiful countryside. Could I buy land and build a vacation home here? Should I buy a condo?*

*Rather than enjoying the peace and the beauty all around me, I was trying to plan a way to take possession of the peace and happiness and own it* ad infinitum. *I am probably safe in saying that most lawyers have an inability to "enjoy "the moment because of a preoccupation with"owning" the moment. It is the equivalent of a child chasing a butterfly because he wants to "have" it, not content to simply appreciate its beauty as it circles overhead.*

*Most lawyers have limited time to spend at snow-covered mountain resorts. Quickie vacations are the most that many of us can hope for. As a result, we want to own the thing that makes us happy during our brief reprieve. It is uncommon for most Type A personality lawyers to stop and smell flowers as we walk through a meadow. Chances are, we are calculating a way to buy the real estate on which that meadow sits.*

## LEARNING TO TRAVEL LIGHT

Another characteristic that is attributed to the Sage is that he or she does not encumber enjoyment of the moment with a selfish desire to forever own the moment. The Sage knows that there never has been and never will be a "scarcity" of joy. There is no scarcity of circumstances, incidents, occasions, occurrences, events, and possessions that can bring us endless joy—provided we are able to move on from joy to joy. The Sage seems to recognize that in order to move from joy to joy, you can't carry all of them with you. There are an endless number of picturesque mountainside views to experience and appreciate without having any ownership interest in them.

In the chapter of his autobiography entitled "Learning to Loaf," Darrow describes a trip to Europe. He writes of visiting "lands where everyone seemed to enjoy joy." He describes his memories of shopkeepers who would close down their shop for noonday meals taking plenty of time to "eat and drink." He writes:

> *No body of working men in Continental Europe are so poor that they cannot sit on the sidewalks with bread and cheese and a bottle of wine, and eat and drink and visit and laugh and talk time away.*

These small joys appealed to Darrow in ways that many upwardly mobile lawyers never grasp. We cannot capture joy, take it home as a trophy, or bring it down with a silver bullet.

We must outgrow the child's emphasis on Christmas-like events. A Sage recognizes that Christmas morning occurs once a year and leaves a long space in between that, for him, is anything but a dry spell. We shouldn't wait for joy to call on us once a year; instead we can look for joy all year long.

## MAKING ROOM FOR JOY

In order to accomplish this we have to "make room" in our lives for joy. In the '70s, the Byrds adapted song lyrics from part of Chapter 3 of Ecclesiastes, fashioning a Top 10 hit of their record "Turn! Turn! Turn!" The words they borrowed from Ecclesiastes are these: "To everything there is a season and a time to every purpose under heaven." Hidden in the lines from the Old Testament and the Byrds hit is the idea that we should make room in our busy lawyering lives for joy and reserve for ourselves a time not only to plant, but a a time to reap the rewards of our labor—leave a time to dance, a time for peace, a time to laugh, a time for silence. Making time for joy requires more courage than most lawyers are able to muster. It is improbable that we will be willing to reserve a season for dancing, peace, laughter, and silence if we are overwhelmed by fear that the rest of the pack is too close to our heels or too far out ahead of us. The Sage abandons a pack mentality. Before raising the objection that most lawyers don't have a pack mentality, think how many of us fashion our lives according to a pre-packaged formula of what a lawyer's life *should* look like.

If you are a defense lawyer for large corporations and insurance companies, can you, with a straight face, suggest that you are not working, dressing, speaking, thinking, seeing, acting, and in general living like those who came before you and those who now work with you? Can most plaintiff's trial lawyers truthfully suggest that they somehow march to the beat of a drum that is substantially different from the cadence heard by most fellow plaintiff's lawyers?

Most of us believed that in becoming a lawyer, we would be able to claim true autonomy. We believed that our degrees and subsequent careers would allow us freedom to live according to the change of seasons that we would choose. By our fifth or sixth year as lawyers, we discovered that our "changes of season" are exactly the same as those of the rest of the pack. Clarence Darrow, however, did not have a pack mentality. He was not as predictable as the phases of the moon. He roamed the hills of his life freely, finding pleasure where it lay. He had the courage to turn a blind eye on the rest of the pack, and follow his own path. After studying the life of Darrow for years, Irving Stone said of him:

> *He was no respecter of sacred cows. The more sacred the cow, the more he believed it needed to be shot at, for every time a man accepted a sacred cow, he closed off still another portion of his brain.*

Stone describes Darrow as a lawyer who worked extremely hard, but he says that when he left his office "he considered himself free, free to write, lecture, debate, and study"—all things that brought Darrow joy. He was indifferent about what he "ought to be doing" as a successful lawyer.

## A CIRCLE OF FRIENDS

Clarence Darrow loved people. The Sage recognizes the benefits of friendship and companionship. Eating, drinking, and enjoying the fruits of our labor are not all that rewarding when we choose to go it alone, without good friends and companions. Darrow's circle of friends and acquaintances was huge. They were politically radical; they were politically conservative; they were Bohemian intellectuals; they were rough and rugged union labor bosses; they were the haves and the have-nots.

It was not common for Darrow to dislike people based on where they stood politically or socially. He was willing to call most people friend and ignore their association with any particular cause. If the success of a person's life can be judged according to the size of his circle of good friends, then Darrow was immensely successful.

Many lawyers within our ranks these days do not devote much time to fostering friendships *inside,* much less outside, their narrowly confined world of lawyering. Consider these comments by Pat Keahey, a lawyer practicing in Birmingham, Alabama:

*Almost from the day I graduated from law school, I began a process of posturing, rattling sabers, and strapping on my armor to deal with the endless conflict I was confronted with as a lawyer. It is difficult to live with such a mentality and, at the same time, foster meaningful friendships inside or outside your professional world. You begin surrounding yourself with colleagues, not friends. It is easy to begin isolating yourself from people who do not in some way help you further your career. It is easy to rationalize that there is simply not enough time to take away from your career. We must bring in business. There are trials to prepare for. There is money to make. There are things to buy for myself and my family. It is not a setting that is conducive to being a good friend or companion.*

Most of us are involved in the daily struggle of lawyering that isolates us from those who are not involved in the struggle with us. Lawyering interferes in several ways with our ability to develop and maintain relationships. Our profession is heavily laden with rivalry, competition, and antagonism. One day we may be engaged in a struggle with some opposing counsel, and the next day we may be at odds with our own partners over some business disagreement. Seldom are we far removed from rivalry in some form or fashion.

The typical lawyer spends ten hours of his twenty-four hour day isolated in a "me against them" mode. Not much time is left to switch gears to a mode amenable to developing and maintaining relationships.

## OUR MAN-MADE EMOTIONS

The Sage does not need to constantly *switch* modes in order to move between his relationships with friends and his relationships with adversaries. Confucian scholars have a term that describes how the "superior person" or Sage interacts with both friend and foe. It is called *jen,* and is explained as a means granting the same quality of attention to both anger or joy, without undue emphasis on either.

The Confucian honors the emotion that he *chooses* to honor, with the goal of treating all people—friend or foe—in a way that reflects the way he wishes to be treated. The notion is that he may control with precision the course of interaction between friend or foe. If he *chooses* to interject anger into the interaction, for instance, he expects that anger to become pivotal and magnified throughout the relationship.

The same holds true for kindness, mean-spiritedness, humility, arrogance, selfishness, unselfishness, and all the other positive and negative human emotions. With *jen,* emotions are at the disposal of the individual rather than disposing of the individual. The Confucian Sage chooses the path of *jen* because he believes that appreciation of life begins by appreciating the other fellow, and *jen* helps him find an approach for doing this.

There are concepts similar to *jen* that are common to other great religious traditions. The Hindu teaches the wisdom of *karma,* the Christian tells us to love our enemies. Linear thinking sometimes does not allow us to gain the full benefit of what these great ideas offer. Application of those truths benefits us far more than it benefits our opponent.

Clarence Darrow was impressed with a simple epitaph that his hero Voltaire left for us to think about: "I died . . . loving my friends [and] not hating my enemies." Like Voltaire, Darrow had more than his share of enemies. Like Voltaire, Darrow chose not to waste time, energy, and spirit despising his enemies and plotting their undoing with some sweet revenge. For Darrow and Voltaire—and the rest of us—there is self-saving benefit in such a philosphy.

The ancient Persian poet Rumi wrote a poem entitled "Ali in Battle." In it Rumi tells the story of how Ali had fought and overcome a powerful knight. The knight, lying helpless on the ground, spat into Ali's face. Ali dropped his sword and helped his opponent to his feet. The astonished knight, expecting to die, asked Ali: "Why have you spared me? How has lightning contracted back into its cloud?" Ali answered:

*I am God's Lion, not the lion of passion . . . When a wind of personal reaction comes, I do not go along with it. There are many winds full of anger and lust and greed. They move the rubbish around, but the solid mountain of our true nature stays where it has always been.*

Darrow understood the wisdom of fighting the good fight without allowing himself to be blown away like rubbish by the winds of "personal reaction."

## WHEN TO THINK ABOUT *JEN*

By the time you finish reading this book, you will, more than likely, have received a phone call, a letter, or a fax from an attorney who is an opponent in one of your many legal skirmishes. Your opponent may be arrogant, egotistical, uncompromising, possibly even flagrantly dishonest. Her goal will be to take advantage of you and your client. She will attempt to make you believe that she is a better, more powerful, more influential lawyer than you. If you allow it, she will become your rival, your foe. She will dredge up every negative human emotion you have pounding away in your heart. She will fill your life with so much anger that you will be left with very little room or energy for friendship and companionship when you leave your office. If that happens, she has "won."

## WHEN BARNS ARE NEVER BIG ENOUGH

The Sage understands the parable of the rich fool. It is a simple parable that most of us understand in principle, but ignore in the way we live as lawyers. It is the story of a very fortunate, wealthy farmer who had so much grain to store that his barns would not hold it all. So he decided to tear down his smaller barns and build bigger barns. It was his belief that once he finally had enough grain stored away, he could sit back and relax, take the time to eat, drink, and be joyful. The parable goes on to pose the obvious question: For whom is he storing all that grain? Does it really make much sense for him to wait until all his barns are filled before he begins to relax and enjoy life? How much of the grain can he take with him when he checks out? Through this parable, Jesus taught his disciples that life is not a "dress rehearsal." He taught that we only have one shot at this process called living, and it doesn't make much sense to spend too much time building bigger barns and storing grain when building bigger barns and storing grain does not leave time for matters of the spirit. The last line in the parable, reported in the New Testament book of Luke, is this: "Where your treasure is, there will your heart be also."

Many lawyers could candidly admit that most of their treasure is in the bank, in stocks, in the things they own. It is not likely that any of us could stomach the idea of giving away *any* of our money or toys, much less all of our worldly possessions, in order to bring better spiritual balance to our lives. But the parable of the rich fool does not suggest that we shave our heads, strap on sandals, and wander around in some

faraway desert, penniless and completely disconnected from the material world. It suggests, however, that hoarding things will not bring us much
joy. It suggests that affection for impersonal things
and inanimate objects diminishes our ability to feel
compassion for people. We begin treating people
with the same detachment with which we treat
things.

Darrow did not struggle much with the question
of "how much is enough?" In fact, he was quick
to brag about the fact that he was not a wealthy
lawyer. He always had enough to live comfort-
ably. He was able to travel throughout most of
Europe several times. He could afford to "spend"
time writing books and lecturing. He merely used
money as a tool to accomplish these things. Nothing about his life suggests that he believed that more
possessions would make him happy. He did not
hoard money or material things. He did not delay
or defer living a full, rewarding, joyful life while
he put more grain in the barn. Thoreau said that a
wise man, given the choice between time and
money, will always choose time. Clarence Darrow
seemed to wholeheartedly agree.

Once a year legal periodicals and journals such as the *National Law Journal,* and the *ABA Journal* tally the incomes of a select few of our brother and sister lawyers. They report that in Houston, Texas, a plaintiff's lawyer made a "gazillion" dollars or, in Washington, D.C., some corporate defense firm has an income equivalent to a small Third World country. It seems valid that an article attempting to evaluate "How much is enough?" would be more beneficial to lawyers everywhere, and would be a sensible inclusion in these journals.

In defense of the journals and their choice of articles, we can say that the editorial content merely reflects what we as lawyers value—what we have become. Information about who can buy what gives us a basis for comparison so that we may decide where we are on that scale of "success." Darrow's name, by the way, would not at any time in his career have made such a list.

## TOO MUCH STUFF

Sometime before Henry David Thoreau went to live in a cabin at Walden Pond, he had discovered something very important about "things." He had learned that each thing we own takes up room in our lives, that having too many things detracts from our enjoyment of life. An admirer of Thoreau's sent a gift to him at Walden Pond, a rug "perfect" for his front porch. Thoreau returned the rug, however, saying: "I came here to lessen my considerations. I already sweep off the stoop. I do not wish to sweep off the stoop *and* shake out the rug."

The idea that less is more was certainly not the intellectual property of Thoreau. American Indians had "giving away" ceremonies, believing that each thing owned claimed a portion of the owner's spirit. The Cheyenne brave who had accumulated too many ponies would give away some of them for the purpose of retaking his spirit and unburdening his physical life. The Sage, whether from Thoreau's rational point of view or a Cheyenne's mystical understanding, keeps his mind free from the distraction of too much "stuff."

Answers to questions like these seem important: Do I really need a bigger barn? Do I need to store more grain before I begin enjoying my life to the fullest? Has the quality of life for me and my family suffered because we don't have enough things?

You are likely to find that quality of life suffers not because you don't have enough. It is probable that your quality of life suffers because you have spent too much time and energy, too much of your life and your family's life, gathering more grain and building bigger barns. The Sage recognizes the advantages of living *now* with what she has rather than waiting for the moment when she can begin living—the moment when she has enough to relax and "enjoy life."

John Acuff calls himself a "country lawyer." He has practiced law for twenty years in Tennessee. He shares these thoughts about hunting and gathering.

*It took a decade or more practicing law before I recognized that things I could afford did not make me or my family happy. When I was making $40,000 per year, I was* *sure I would be happier if only I could make $50,000 per year. When I made $50,000, I was sure I could be happier if only I could make $60,000 and so on, and so on.*

*Nowadays I try to borrow some of the good formulas for living that many of my clients have shown me. For example, in my practice I do a certain amount of estate planning. I see farmers and their wives of 40 or 50 years come into my office wearing clean but well-worn work clothes, happily married, holding hands, and looking just thrilled to have each other and their family. Typically, they ask me to draw up a will to include their 150 to 300 acres of good farmland, usually "bought and paid for"; they are driving a pickup that is paid for; and they have half a million dollars in CDs. Most of their wealth and happiness is a result of limiting their needs and living within their means.*

*What is most impressive, however, is the attitude that prevails with these people. They are comfortable with their place in the world and the possessions they own. Unlike so many lawyers I know who run themselves ragged jockeying for a better place in the fast lane, lawyers who still have not figured out that more, bigger, shinier, and newer is not necessarily better, these farmers I am talking about are blessed with a clear vision of what really matters, about what is really important, and because of that they live their lives in a better, a more sensible way."*

Lawyering sometimes takes us to a place where we begin to believe that wealth and affluence sufficient to really satisfy us is only one case away, one more year away, one more deal away.

## ALL THE WORLD'S A STAGE

*EXIT, STAGE RIGHT*

The Sage sees an advantage in sometimes doing nothing. Blaise Pascal, a French religious scholar, mathematician, and philosopher, said that most of the problems of mankind stem from our inability to sit alone in a room with nothing to do. He believed that most people have an inability to deeply and quietly know themselves.

Most lawyers do not schedule much time for quiet or solitude into the frenzy of lawyering. The Sage, however, understands that there must be—amid all the tendency to overachieve, overdo, outdo, one-up, and grandstand—consciously chosen, waking time when we do absolutely nothing. A time to take up and a time to put down. A time to jump off the warhorse, take off the helmet, drop the saber, sit down, and deeply exhale in a long, slow breath all the worry and tension that comes with what we have chosen to do.

These quiet times spent emptying the mind of all its clutter and rattle and hum is time spent caring for the spirit. And, for the Sage, a strong and healthy spirit is the rock upon which is built his lawyering, his personal relationships, and his avocational pursuits. He knows there'll always be a flood of unexpected difficulties, from flat tires to client woes. Whether one is carried off thrashing and drowning in the torrent, or left firmly rooted until things subside a bit, is decided by one's ability to claim an internal calm. Controlling the external stuff is way outside our domain.

Clarence Darrow knew that the "world out there" seems sometimes outright oblivious of our presence:

> *What we call time rolls on its course and in the twinkle of an eye turns puppets into oblivions regardless of how wildly they shout that the multitude may know that they are here.*

Implicit in Darrow's comment is the advice to not become a puppet, tossed about willy-nilly, to and fro, at the whim of whatever capricious character or circumstance is pulling your strings. Besides, it is a waste of effort to be forever shouting to be recognized and acknowledged. The lawyering job description certainly calls for at least some shouting, but it makes more sense to do like the banker we described earlier—do the shouting without becoming the shout. It is not easy, though, in this business, to be alone, unnoticed, and temporarily disconnected from the fray. Especially since many of us chose a lawyering career because we enjoy, even *adore,* the spotlight at center stage more than most other people. Unfortunately after several curtain calls, so to speak, we become convinced that the entire play will close down amid boos and financial collapse if we step backstage for even a scene or two.

The truth is that your brief exits will do you and the whole show nothing but good. For most of us, this drama called lawyering is a long ten-hour day, every day. Even if the show won't go on unless you are front and center 90 percent of the time, that still leaves an hour you can call your own. *Take it!* Claim it when and while you can.

We have got to learn to accept the idea that quiet contemplation does much to improve our lives as lawyers. World War II commanders of warships in the British navy were taught to delay for a full minute before executing a tactical response to a missile or torpedo strike. The theory was that a "disciplined delay" could prevent a foolish, hasty call by the commander. Laying back a bit before engaging the enemy is hard to do when we have become addicted to being heard and seen standing tall in the middle of the fracas. A call for a moment's meditation makes many among our ranks real uneasy.

In Taoist thought, a sage understands and lives by *wu wei,* a Taoist principle that suggests the right course of action sometimes is "no action." *Wu wei* is a conscious decision to do nothing. It should not be mistaken for passivity. The Taoist would describe *wu wei* as "action through non-action," or "doing by not doing." If we cannot get into the idea of rest for rest's sake in the middle of a lawyering day, at least we can agree with the British navy and Taoist sages that in many instances the correct action is to take no action. A rabbit, for example, who wants to cross a busy highway during the height of rush hour is better off taking action by non-action. His non-action puts him in better harmony with the world around him, which, at that moment, is filled with hot rubber, gas fumes, impatient drivers, and a million cars whizzing across his path. The rabbit is obviously better off sitting motionless by the side of that busy highway and waiting for circumstances to change.

Most lawyers' idea of non-action is a quickie vacation. We schedule a respite in some lovely setting for the purpose of stepping back from the consuming flames of our practice. We schedule such times for taking a rest, for relaxing, and for letting our minds wander aimlessly—sometimes to fantasies about doing something other than lawyering. But fourteen days deftly pinched from three hundred sixty-five days of turmoil and stress will hardly fill the bill for "finding some peace."

The Sage doesn't rely on a brief hiatus at a sunny beach in Cozumel for his moment's peace. Seeking peace for the Sage is an everyday ritual—part of his daily "liturgy." He understands that his needs for peace are better served by the solitude found behind a closed office door, while the fray of business spins crazily on just outside. Thirty minutes or an hour of enforced, peaceful silence—no phones or visitors, with business on hold—is like a change in seasons. His non-action takes him from a sweltering August to a cool April.

The back jacket of biographer Irving Stone's *Darrow for the Defense* says of Clarence Darrow that he dissipated "his magnificent energies through a killing pace of work." Darrow took his pleasure, but took it on the fly. There finally came a time when he allowed himself to learn to loaf a bit.

*I did not want any longer to fight in a courthouse all day and study and contrive far into the night, and be back in the courtroom at ten in the morning after a troublous sleep. I wanted to get up when I wished and stay at home all day if I wished, and read some of the books in my library that I had always intended to enjoy but could not. . . . So I determined to close my office door and call it my day's work. Or a life work. . . . It was high time that I should begin to stroll peacefully and pleasantly toward the end of the trail, which, at best, must be but a little way beyond.*

Don't wait until the end of the trail to begin "closing your office door," "staying at home all day," or "strolling peacefully." Engage in non-action. Have the courage to go unnoticed, unheard. Intentionally and routinely take a position far to the right of center stage—out of shouting distance.

Darrow must have withdrawn at times to recharge his spiritual and intellectual batteries, or else he would not have been able to keep up his "killing pace" for half a century and more. Even Jesus, who, the Gospels tell us, was another hard worker, took time to nap along the road between "engagements." He is reported to have frequently withdrawn from the crowds. All the great religions share the same advice to their faithful to take time in solitude to meditate and pray. Buddha became enlightened during a solitary spell sitting beneath a tree. He also "took off" the entire three-month rainy season every year for the whole forty-five years he taught. Mohammed would "go to the mountain." Clarence Darrow must have grabbed for himself regular "retreat" moments when working, though neither he nor his biographers tell us he did. I would, however, bet on it.

## MOVING THROUGH THE STAGES

The life of the Sage is one of continual evolution toward greater spiritual maturity. His transformation probably has not been some touchy-feely mystical conversion, but rather the product of conscious effort and hard work—what Buddha called *right effort.* "Work out your own salvation with diligence," the Buddha declared.

Our Sage has not been given wisdom in the way a cartoon character gets a bright idea when a light bulb flashes on above his head. He did not enlighten his life by memorizing a collection of prepackaged "thoughts for the day," or "virtues to live by." Instead, he was willing, all along, to do the "heavy lifting." William James said enlightenment is the the result of the "slow dull heave of the will." The Sage, for the sake of his spirit, has been willing to close the doors of his office early on occasion, to cancel appointments and turn his attention away from deadlines and dollars, the competition for material things. Outside his office door the power and influence struggles continue—acquistions and getting ahead dominate the thinking. The struggle to "be there" and "look out for number one" goes on uninterrupted.

Inside his office, however, something far different is going on. Behind those closed doors he is using some of his valuable time and energy to stay in touch with what he regards as his higher self—a self whose voice often gets lost. He is thinking the unthinkable, that perhaps there is a better way to live and lawyer, with benefits not only for him, but for his spouse, his children, his partners, his clients, and his entire community.

Robert Johnson in his book *Transformations* explains how very difficult it is and how very few people will actually accomplish the full "interior journey" toward maturity of the spirit.

Johnson writes:

> *Tradition indicates that three levels of consciousness are available to us: simple consciousness, not often seen in our modern technological world; complex consciousness, the usual state of educated Western man; and an enlightened state of consciousness, known only to a very few individuals, which is the culmination of human evolution and can be attained only by highly motivated people after much work and training.*

Johnson's tone of pessimism about the likelihood of many actually making the transformation to that state that he calls the highest level of consciousness grows out of what he sees as misplaced priorities in our culture and society. The journey of transformation toward spiritual maturity is made difficult because many of the values and images that we center our lives on are so deeply entrenched in our hearts and minds. Johnson suggests that we are unwilling to "transform" our consciousness because our egotistical interest in image preservation and devotion to "stuff" makes change improbable.

By the time the typical lawyer makes it from his bed to his desk he has already been inundated with hundreds of messages from the marketing mavens of Madison Avenue telling him what car to drive, where to vacation, how he should smell and look and dress, even how he will be thinking if he is a "man on the go and in the know." But nowhere among the millions of advertisements he has been bombarded with since he was a kid watching Saturday morning cartoons has there ever been one that questioned the sense of buying more stuff. Madison Avenue has always been and remains in the business of selling soap, so to speak, not maturity of the spirit.

A brilliant renegade academic, Andrew Bard Schmookler, argues in his book *Fool's Gold— The Fate of Values in a World of Goods* that, on one hand, the things that religions for centuries have taught people to avoid—excessive attachment to possessions, and enslavement to our whims and desires—are the very things that advertising, on the other hand, teaches us to "go for" with all of our time, and every dollar we have, and every ounce of energy we can muster. He writes that industry and advertising have diverted "the deepest spiritual values of our culture from the realm of the sacred to the goods they [peddle]."

Schmookler traces this notion as far back as 1928, to an ad in *Printers Ink Monthly*. The advertisement said that advertisements were "beginning to occupy the place in inspiration that religion did several hundred years ago." Schmookler points to a 1971 study that found, for instance, that among a sampling of U. S. citizens 43 percent of them regarded "completely true" the advertising slogan "Perfect rice every time."

If anything, our gullibility has grown worse in the twenty-five years since that study. But the Sage ain't buyin' "perfect rice." He doesn't have to because the unhealthy ego center that the advertisers so easily manipulate does not control the Sage. The community that Sol Linowitz says we are responsible for does not care about the kind of car we drive, the style and brand of clothes we wear, where we live or how much real estate we own. They do not care about our inventory of expensive possessions, or anything that we "have." Our communities do, however, care about what we have in our hearts. It matters very much to them whether or not we lawyers occupy the same spiritual high ground that Clarence Darrow occupied.

It should be reasonably apparent to most of us that the public does not believe that we walk the same high ground Darrow walked. They do not believe our hearts beat to the same rhythm as Clarence Darrow's. It is also true that while the public's perception of lawyers is not entirely our doing, we have done more than our share to generate such a poor public image. Ralph Nader and Wesley J. Smith in 1996 published a compelling book entitled *No Contest*, which paints a not-too-pretty picture of lawyering as a profession upside-down with a caliber of greed, arrogance, and dishonesty that is approaching moral bankruptcy.

Nader and Smith offer us a wake-up call, giving us true-to-life examples of attorneys who have lost their souls in the process of becoming rich and powerful. Their book provides example after example of lawyers who have shown an almost Faustian willingness to sacrifice spiritual values—or what should at least be "core" values—in exchange for power and material gain. *No Contest* is an agonizingly candid indictment of our profession. It is a book that puts into perspective how dim Darrow's honorable and high-minded spirit has become in the eyes of too many within our ranks.

For Clarence Darrow, some money was just to expensive. Darrow's home, his car and clothes, his things, were not purchased at a price "too high" for his soul to afford. Greed and love of power and influence were not impediments to enlightened living for Darrow. Free of those chains, he was free to become a Sage.

*Oh, pooh!*

*—what does one know about it, anyhow,*

*when he talks about God?*

*—Clarence Darrow*

# Part Eight

## Afterword

Each of the world's great religions offers steps on a path to enlightenment, as described, sought, and known by the faithful followers of Buddhism, Hinduism, Islam, Judaism, Taoism, and Christianity. The very best ideas that these religions have to offer are ideas that are similar to what the Sage has likely relied on to improve the way he lives.

The theologies that support each religion are several and various and, at worst, are divisive and engender conflict and persecution. Possibly for these reasons, and because of a lack of faith in "faith," and a strong emphasis on reason that is supported by *evidence* and sound *logic,* Clarence Darrow never became a churchman, choosing agnosticism instead.

What Darrow had faith in was not organized religion but the force of the ideas and the wisdom that evolved from these various traditions. He wrote that he could not, however, believe in God "because I trust my reason," adding:

> *No man living can form a picture of any God, and you can't believe in an object unless you can form a picture of it. You may believe in the* force, *but not in the object. If there is any God in the universe, I don't know it.*

He was highly critical of belief in mystical, unexplainable phenomena and found them to be far-fetched and contrary to reason. The "force" behind religious experience, however, was with him in the way he lived his life every day. Darrow admitted to a search of such diligence to find "proof" of the existence of man's soul, that it seems to me born of hope for success:

*So far as having any prejudice against this doctrine [of soul], I have no more desire to disbelieve than I have as to any other theories of a future life. In fact, for many years, I have searched here for evidence. . . . For more than fifty years, until ten years past, I have given some attention to spiritualism.*

*. . . I have for years investigated what are called spiritual phenomena. I am satisfied that if any intelligent man, in possession of his senses, thoroughly investigates spiritualism, he will find that there is no evidence to support his faith.*

It is that word "faith" in the foregoing that is the operative factor for the rest of us who are practitioners of some religion, but which, for Darrow, was a door he would not enter. Faith, by its very definition, cannot be reduced to "Exhibit A." Darrow was a lawyer who needed proof, evidence, exhibits. While "the rest of us" do not go about seeking evidence, neither do we count ourselves gullible and "dispossessed of our senses." For me at least, my faith as a Christian is buoyed up by what I see in the world all around me—not only in nature, but in the historical and contemporary actions of men and women.

Reverend Jim Wallace is a social activist who has spent many years of his life finding ways to clothe, feed, and provide shelter for the homeless in Washington, D.C. This is what he says about faith: "Faith is the act of believing in spite of the evidence, and watching the evidence change."

The type of faith discussed in this book is a faith that tells us there are laws for living that are knocking around in our universe that are no less constant and predictable than the physical laws of nature. For example, we all know in our hearts that when we show compassion, honesty, and decency toward family, friend, or even foe, most of the time we receive the same in our own lives. Accepting and living according to such an idea helps us to live a wiser, more enlightened life.

When he incorporates what he feels in his heart, and knows in his head, with what he does with his hands, the lawyer finds it more difficult to do the bidding of a corrupt corporation. The judge is less likely to allow her position of power—or the "weight of her gavel"—to distort her sense of fairness and decency. If she is wiser and more enlightened, it is reflected in her conduct and behavior. Clarence Darrow said:

> *We are all moved by common impulses and touched by mutual understanding. We gain kinship with the world. . . . No one can feel this universal relationship without being gentler, kindlier, and more humane toward all the infinite forms of beings that live with us, and must die with us.*

This *understanding* that Darrow acquired as a Journeyman allowed him to be gentler, kindlier, and more humane. It is the same kind of understanding that the world's religious traditions seek to engender.

Places of worship continue to exist. They have not gone out of style—not even among Darrow-caliber intellectuals—because there is another part of our nature, equally as important as our individuality, that welcomes the possibility of gathering together in a place of worship with others who are generally of a similar mind. That part of our nature is the part that seeks community with others. It is the same part of ourselves that finds joy in serving someone, something, besides our own selfish interests. It is the part of us that from time to time seeks spiritual renewal.

It is the common *experience* of people towards a meaning and purpose greater than their own ego-charged goals that motivates them, I believe, to come together within their temples, mosques, synagogues, and churches to worship and learn together. That does not mean that the faithful check their intelligence at the front door the way gunslingers did when they entered a well-marshalled saloon. They know that their mosques and temples are homes to many ideas they don't share.

Most people who practice a formal brand of religion are not looking for a "perfect" church where they will find total agreement with all its doctrines and dogma, all its rituals and liturgy, all its clergymen and theologians. It has been and will remain impossible to come up with a universal theology. No matter how desirable the common goal, people will not submit to a beehive mentality regarding any idea, much less religion. Clarence Darrow would, I believe, say that human recalcitrancy is good. Chinese philospher Lin Yutang said, "Cows and dictators go well together—dictators and monkeys do not." Darrow wisely pressed people to use their reason, to employ tools of intellect and logic to arrive at reasonable beliefs that are distinctly not of the hand-me-down variety.

*So long as men think and feel, at least some of them will use their faculties [for logical contemplation]. For if we are to believe*

> *things that are not true, who is to write our creed? Is it safe to leave any man or organization to pick out the errors we must accept? The whole history of the world has answered this question in a way that cannot be mistaken.*

It has not been my intent in this book to suggest that we abandon the type of "logical contemplation" that Clarence Darrow put to such good use in his life as a Journeyman. I merely suggest that we remove a few bumps and potholes in the road we travel down as Journeymen, and that may be done by paying attention to the many well-drawn road maps left for us by the wisdom traditions.

Logical contemplation should lead us to the conclusion that we need to do better for ourselves and the community we serve. We need to pay attention to some of the simple ideas about wiser and enlightened living that echo in the halls of our temples, mosques, synagogues, and churches. We need to show no less faith in spiritual laws for living than we do in the physical laws of this world.

These spiritual laws are dressed up differently according to where you go looking for them. But, if we look a little closer, they all give us similar ideas about how we can do better. One religious community may guide us toward empathy by telling us to love our family, friends, and neighbors and to treat them in a way that we would want to be loved and treated. Another religious community might remind us of the *karma* we create for ourselves as a result of the way we treat others. The point is, it is religion particularly that constantly reminds us how we should be treating the community of people we are supposed to be serving. It is our religious traditions that provide a method for carving out of our busy lives a consistent place and time for remembering the ideas that become a "force" to help us become better lawyers—and how to become Journeymen, Teachers, Servants, possibly even Sages.

For me, I have found not a perfect but a suitable place within the Methodist Church to go for "remembering" the things I know—and have always known—that will ultimately grant me a good night's sleep. By that I mean that when I review my conduct with and toward all the "others" whom I have lawyered for and against, am I able to feel a sense of peace about that conduct? Am I able to conclude that I have done at least tolerably well against the standard of how I would like to have been treated myself? And if not, can I do better tomorrow?

In my church, I am reminded of all these simple rules, which any teenager can understand, but which often seem so evasive in the "real world" of lawyering. The rules, the "winnowed wisdom of the human race," as Huston Smith put it, are not aphorisms that we can commit to memory and thereby simply find ourselves behaving at all times like little Buddhas or little Christs.

All I suggest in this book is that it we may make a consistent effort to live by the force of ideas contained within that "winnowed wisdom." It is that effort that I consider to be part of the Journeyman lawyer's job description. But it is also an effort that will help us overcome aspects of living as a lawyer that cause what we do with